NEWCAS   ⌣ᴇʀIES: 2

DAVID CONSTANTINE:
A LIVING LANGUAGE

NEWCASTLE/BLOODAXE POETRY SERIES

1: Linda Anderson & Jo Shapcott (eds.)
Elizabeth Bishop: Poet of the Periphery

2: David Constantine: *A Living Language:*
NEWCASTLE / BLOODAXE POETRY LECTURES

NEWCASTLE/BLOODAXE POETRY LECTURES

In this innovative series of public lectures at the University of Newcastle upon Tyne, leading contemporary poets speak about the craft and practice of poetry to audiences drawn from both the city and the university. The lectures are then published in book form by Bloodaxe, giving readers everywhere the opportunity to learn what the poets themselves think about their own subject.

Forthcoming titles in this series include lectures given at Newcastle by Jo Shapcott, Fred D'Aguiar and Carol Rumens.

NEWCASTLE/BLOODAXE POETRY SERIES: 1

DAVID CONSTANTINE

A Living Language

NEWCASTLE / BLOODAXE POETRY LECTURES

Copyright © David Constantine 2003, 2004

ISBN: 1 85224 688 X

First published 2004 by
Department of English Literary & Linguistic Studies,
University of Newcastle,
Newcastle upon Tyne NE1 7RU,
in association with
Bloodaxe Books Ltd,
Highgreen,
Tarset,
Northumberland NE48 1RP.

www.bloodaxebooks.com
For further information about Bloodaxe titles
please visit our website or write to
the above address for a catalogue.

Bloodaxe Books Ltd acknowledges
the financial assistance of
Arts Council England, North East.

LEGAL NOTICE
All rights reserved. No part of this book may be
reproduced, stored in a retrieval system, or
transmitted in any form, or by any means, electronic,
mechanical, photocopying, recording or otherwise,
without prior written permission from Bloodaxe Books Ltd.
Requests to publish work from this book
must be sent to Bloodaxe Books Ltd.
David Constantine has asserted his right under
Section 77 of the Copyright, Designs and Patents Act 1988
to be identified as the author of this work.

Cover printing by J. Thomson Colour Printers Ltd, Glasgow.

Printed in Great Britain by
Bell & Bain Limited, Glasgow, Scotland.

Contents

Translation Is Good for You   *7*
Use and Ornament   *26*
Poetry of the Present   *42*

Translation Is Good for You

Even in a life as short and a development as rapid as Keats's still it is possible to say: then came a breakthrough. There was one in October 1816. Keats, training to be a surgeon, was becoming more and more sure of his real vocation. Typically, he decided it not just by solitary reading and writing but in the society of friends. Charles Cowden Clarke, the son of the headmaster at Keats's school in Enfield and his friend and mentor there, had by 1816 actively sought him out again and taken him up into his own lively circle. He promised to introduce him to Leigh Hunt, a celebrated and influential man in the world of letters. Keats was eager for the meeting. He wrote (*Letters*, p. 7): ' 't will be an Era in my existance', using the word to mean the point of departure into a new phase. But before that occasion came another, again through the agency of Cowden Clarke and equally fit to be and to mark an era. Keats alludes to it in the same letter: 'From a few Words of yours when last I saw you, I have no doubt but that you have something in your Portfolio which I should by rights see...' That something was a copy of Chapman's Homer, borrowed by Clarke from Thomas Massa Alsager and to be shared with Keats. The first intention seems to have been that Clarke should come to Keats with the book. Keats gives him directions to his lodgings in Dean Street, then an insalubrious and rather unsafe neighbourhood and now obliterated under London Bridge Station. They thought better of it, the book was too rare and valuable to risk through those streets. Keats came to Clarke in Clerkenwell, for the evening. They read all night. The whole occasion was one of extraordinary presence. First the book itself, the rare substantial folio of 1616, containing *The Whole Works of Homer; Prince of Poetts in his Iliads and Odysses. Translated according to the Greeke, by Geo: Chapman* – the rough pages, the old script, brought into immediate life by Cowden Clarke, a big man with a notably strong voice. He read aloud, Keats listened.

Long after his death, Clarke remembered how Keats looked while he listened: 'How distinctly is that earnest stare, and protrusion of the upper lip now present to me, as we came upon some piece of rough-hewn doric elevation in the fine old poet.' And the liveliest detail of all: 'He sometimes shouted...'. Clarke read from the *Iliad*, Book III, a passage in which, appropriately, the power of Ithacus' oratory is described; from Book V, the shield and helmet of Diomedes; and, from Book XIII, these lines relating the arrival of Neptune among the Greek ships:

> He clothed himselfe. The golden scourge (most elegantly done)
> He tooke and mounted to his seate, and then the God begun
> To drive his chariot through the waves. From whirlepits every way
> The whales exulted under him and knew their king: the Sea
> For joy did open, and his horse so swift and lightly flew
> The under-axeltree of brasse no drop of water drew.
> And thus these deathless Coursers brought their king to th'Achive ships.
>   Twixt th'Imber Cliffs and Tenedos a certaine Caverne creepes
> Into the deepe sea's gulphie breast, and there th'earth-shaker staid
> His forward steeds, tooke them from coach and heavenly fodder laid
> In reach before them.

These are George Chapman's famous 'fourteeners'; for the *Odyssey* he tried a tighter line, the iambic pentameter. This passage from Book V in which the shipwrecked Odysseus arrives more dead than alive on the blessed island of King Alcinous, pleased Keats especially. Indeed, says Clarke, 'the sea had soakt his heart through' (for which, incidentally, there is no basis in the Greek) had 'the reward of one of his delighted stares':

> This (though but spoke in thought) the Godhead heard,
> Her Current strait staid, and her thicke waves cleard
> Before him, smooth'd her waters, and just where
> He praid, half drownd, entirely sav'd him there.
>   Then forth he came, his both knees faltring, both
> His strong hands hanging downe, and all with froth
> His cheeks and nosthrils flowing, voice and breath
> Spent to all use; and downe he sunke to Death.
> The sea had soakt his heart through: all his vaines
> His toiles had rackt t'a labouring woman's paines.
> Dead wearie was he.

Keats left 'at the day-spring' and walked the two or three miles home, in 'a teeming wonderment', so Clarke says. At 8 Dean Street he sat down at once, took a sheet of paper, marked out the guiding rhyme-scheme, and with only one alteration ('deep brow'd' for 'low brow'd' in l. 6) wrote the sonnet 'On the first looking into Chapman's Homer'; sealed it in an envelope with no other word, hailed a messenger and sent it over to Clarke's address. Clarke, coming down for breakfast at 10 o'clock, opened his post and read:

> Much have I travell'd in the Realms of Gold,
> And many goodly States and Kingdoms seen,
> Round many Western islands have I been
> Which Bards in fealty to Apollo hold.
> Oft of one wide expanse had I been told,
> Which deep brow'd Homer ruled as his Demesne:
> Yet could I never judge what Men could mean,
> Till I heard Chapman speak out loud and bold.
>
> Then felt I like some Watcher of the Skies
> When a new Planet swims into his Ken,
> Or like stout Cortez, when with wondr'ing eyes
> He star'd at the Pacific, and all his Men
> Look'd at each other with a wild surmise –
> Silent upon a Peak in Darien.

The sonnet, his most assured to date, is both the mark of an era and an era in itself. The imagery – from astronomy (he alludes to Herschel's discovery of Uranus) and from voyages of discovery (he conflates or confuses Cortes and Balboa) – expresses the particular excitement of a new advance in reading, which itself becomes an image of the new era in his existence as his poetic life gets confidently under way. The agent is a translation, an act of carrying over and passing on. The epics of the 8th century BC, done into the English of Shakespeare's day and age, are brought to life – aloud – two hundred years later by a man with the voice, the bearing, the vocation (as teacher and friend) to do just such a thing for the good of a poet on the threshold of coming fully into his gifts. Pope's version of Homer could not have done that. It needed the recovery of something by then already archaic ('rough-hewn doric', in Clarke's phrase) for the full novelty of the thing to be brought, with the shock of the foreign, into the present where it could live and work. It is as immediate as could be. Clarke's 'loud and bold' voice aptly speaks out the character of the translation. The effect on Keats is intensely physical – his stare, his shouts – and the response, his conversion of the event into a poem of his own, this takes place in the act of walking home through the waking capital, across the river. He teems like London, he opens like the Thames towards the sea. Then, gift for gift, he sends the poem to his good friend's breakfast table.

There is a sad little coda to this famous story of Keats and Chapman. Preparing for his voyage to Italy in the summer of 1820 – he would embark at Tower Dock – Keats was bothered in all his other business by a note from Benjamin Haydon whom he had got to know, with Homer and Leigh Hunt, in that memorable autumn of 1816. Haydon had been another agent in the enlargement of Keats's life. Now he wrote (14 July 1820): 'Have you done with Chapman's Homer? I want it very badly at this moment; will you let the bearer have it; as well as let me know how you are?' A month, and another note from Haydon, later, Keats had still not returned the borrowed book. It had gone missing from his lodgings. He wrote rather desperately to Taylor and Hessey, to procure him another one. Perhaps they did, or perhaps Haydon's own turned up. Keats concluded his last brief note to that friend: 'At some future time I shall re borrow your Homer' (*Letters*, p. 513).

When Keats did his walking tour through the Lakes and Scotland (June–August 1818) the only reading he took with him was Dante's Divine Comedy in the translation (called *The Vision of Dante*) by Henry Francis Cary, first published entire, in three 32mo volumes, by Taylor and Hessey in 1814. Dante was a known text and point of reference for Keats throughout his short adult life. Dealing with bank managers, for example, he described as 'worse than any thing in Dante' (*Letters*, p. 277). One encounter in particular belongs in this discussion of translation and its good effects. It would not have happened but for a translation (Cary's), and it demonstrates, like the encounter with Homer, Keat's peculiarly quick, sensuous and involved response. It came in April 1819, and the account of it is given in the stupendous letter-journal that Keats wrote, between 14 February and 3 May that year, to his brother George and sister-in-law Georgiana in America. His own words are best:

> The fifth canto of Dante pleases me more and more – it is that one in which he meets with Paulo and Franchesca – I had passed many days in rather a low state of mind, and in the midst of them I dreamt of being in that region of Hell. The dream was one of the most

delightful enjoyments I ever had in my life – I floated about the whirling atmosphere as it is described with a beautiful figure to whose lips mine were joined as it seem'd for an age – and in the midst of all this cold and darkness I was warm – even flowery tree tops sprung up and we rested on them sometimes with the lightness of a cloud till the wind blew us away again.

Thus far the reading has its effect, elicits its response, in a dream, one strange element of which is the conversion of torment into bliss. But Keats could not rest there. The dream, reworking images from Dante to express his troubled psyche, drives him to further expression in a poem. In his letter to George and Georgiana his account of the whole experience continues so:

I tried a Sonnet upon it – there are fourteen lines but nothing of what I felt in it – O that I could dream it every night –

> As Hermes once took to his feathers light
> When lulled Argus, baffled, swoon'd and slept
> So on a delphic reed my idle spright
> So play'd, so charm'd so conquer'd, so bereft
> The dragon world of all its hundred eyes
> And seeing it asleep so fled away: –
> Not to pure Ida with its snow [clad] cold skies,
> Nor unto Tempe where Jove grieved that day,
> But to that second circle of sad hell,
> Where in the gust, the whirlwind and the flaw
> Of Rain and hailstones lovers need not tell
> Their sorrows – Pale were the sweet lips I saw
> Pale were the lips I kiss'd and fair the form
> I floated with about that melancholy storm –
>
> (*Letters*, p. 326)

The sonnet comes to life, lifts into truth, at line 9, where the reading and the dreaming begin to be re-lived. Prior to that, in fanciful periphrasis, and alluding, by way of illustration, to the story of Zeus, Io, Hermes and Argus, he has said that through the power of poetry he was finally able to subdue the worries of the daytime world and escape – and where to? To the second circle of Dante's Hell. That locus in the sonnet is notably less blissful than it is in the preceding prose account. Describing it Keats conflates details from Cary's fifth canto, where the lovers are dashed and whirled for ever down the wind, with his sixth, where the torment is 'showers / Ceaseless, accursed, heavy and cold...Large hail, discoloured water, sleety flaw'. All the stranger then the delicious warmth and lightness he felt in the dream itself. But the truth the psyche is troubled by and in dream and sonnet, after reading Dante, is seeking to express, is actually so contradictory and unstable. By April 1819 Keats was six months or more in love with Fanny Brawne. He wrote the draft of this sonnet in the *Inferno* volume of the Dante he gave her. Love for her, association of himself and her with Paolo and Francesca, who consummated their love (and were damned for it) when they read together of the love of Lancelot and Guinevere – all that surfaced in his reading, his dreaming and his sonnet. That and much more. Through November of the previous year, deeper and deeper in love with Fanny, he was nursing his brother Tom in his final illness. Tom died 1 December, and on Christmas Day Keats and Fanny made a significant – if not formal – advance in their relationship. Keats and George believed that their brother's decline and death had been hastened by a cruel deception played on him by a certain Charles Wells. Wells had led Tom to believe himself loved by and to fall in love with a woman called Amena, who was a fiction of his, Wells's, making. Wells wrote letters to Tom in her name. In the letter to George and Georgiana Keats passes immediately from vowing vengeance on Wells ('I will harm him all I possibly can') to recounting his dream of the Second Circle and copying out his sonnet. The cold in that sonnet (note the alteration in l. 7) and the twice alluded-to pale lips are expressive of Tom's experience of love and death, and anticipate his own. Five days later, with no preamble, Keats continued his letter with the first and almost final draft of 'La Belle Dame Sans Merci'. This famous poem, springing up in the context of the ongoing letter, continues the line of troubled preoccupation with love, a wasting suffering and death. Cary's Dante, Keats's account of his dream in the letter to George and Georgiana, his sonnet, 'La Belle Dame Sans Merci' are all texts along the way. Imagery in his sonnet – the cold, the pale lips – returns yet more killingly in the knight's dream 'on the cold hill's side'. He sees 'pale Kings and Princes too/ Pale warriors death pale were they all'. They are kin to those 'whom love bereaved of life' in the Second Circle; those like Paolo, Francesca, Lancelot, Guinevere whom 'love thralled'. Or like Tom, at the mercy of the fictitious

Amena; or Keats himself, likewise consumptive, likewise in thrall. The interconnections, the welter of coexistent troubling thoughts and feelings, are breathtaking. But that precisely is the truth of the life being lived. We can witness it, in Keats's own phrase (borrowed from *Lear*, at Burns's cottage) 'as if we were God's spies' (*Letters*, p. 178).

Those are two instances of a person being given access to a valuable new zone of reading through the good offices of a translator. Keats's response to Homer and Dante, whom George Chapman and Henry Francis Cary had translated, was exceptionally intense and involved. But every reader must be grateful for what translators open up; and will be affected, altered, shifted, and will respond and reciprocate in some fashion and in some degree. That is the most obvious sense in which translation is good for you. All readers, whether they are themselves writers or not, benefit by having books made available to them out of languages which they cannot read.

Translations are valuable in that they give access. Furthermore, writers who themselves translate, gain by doing so. The practice is good for them; their writing benefits. Keats, not known as a translator, may still prove the point.

At Enfield foreign languages (French and Latin at least) were well taught, and translation was encouraged. Keats, once he had decided to become a good pupil (after the return of his mother, when he was thirteen) forthwith won a prize for a translation of Fénelon and launched into a prose translation of the *Aeneid*. Cowden Clarke thought he did all twelve books, and commented: 'the quantity he wrote of translation during the last 18 months or 2 years of his stay at Enfield was surprising...'. It seems he continued with Virgil, encouraged and perhaps supervised by Clarke, for a further couple of years after leaving school. Certainly Gittings (p. 63) thinks his second translation prize – for the *Aeneid* – was awarded after he had left.

Keats's later dealings with the sixteenth-century French poet Ronsard are of interest here. Considering them may widen our idea of translation and its benefits.

On 10 September 1817, taking an interest in his sister's studies, he said of the French language that it was 'perhaps the poorest one ever spoken since the jabbering in the Tower of Babel'; he wished it would be superseded by Italian 'in every School throughout the Country'. But a year later he borrowed the works of Pierre Ronsard from Richard Woodhouse, appreciated the poems and, in a peculiar fashion, did a translation of one of them. In a letter to Charles Dilke on 21 September 1818, having just amusingly mischaracterised himself as a man with 'a Mind too well regulated to proceed upon any thing without due preliminary remarks', he did just that: 'The following is a translation of a Line of Ronsard – "Love poured her Beauty into my warm veins" – ' Next day he sent John Hamilton Reynolds all but the last two lines of that sonnet, saying: 'Here is a free translation of a Sonnet of Ronsard, which I think will please you – I have the loan of his works – they have great Beauties.' Before we read the translation it will be helpful, as very often with Keats, to consider the context in which he presented it. He was nursing Tom, and the day before had written to Dilke:

> I wish I could say Tom was any better. His identity presses upon me so all day that I am obliged to go out – and although I intended to have given some time to study alone I am obliged to write, and plunge into abstract images to ease my self of his countenance his voice and feebleness – so that I live now in a continual fever – it must be poisonous to life although I feel well.   (*Letters*, p. 216)

Then to Reynolds he added the other ingredient of his state: 'I never was in love – yet the voice and the shape of a Woman has haunted me these two days...Poor Tom – that woman – and Poetry were ringing changes in my senses.' Poetry itself he calls a 'feverous relief'. The woman in question was, probably, Jane Cox; and he was on the threshold of meeting Fanny Brawne; disposed to love her, we might say. The sonnet, 'a free translation', reads:

> Nature withheld Cassandra in the skies,
>   For more adornment, a full thousand years;
> She took their cream of Beauty's fairest dyes,
>   And shap'd and tinted her above all Peers:
> Meanwhile Love kept her dearly with his wings,
>   And underneath their shadow fill'd her eyes
> With such a richness that the cloudy Kings
>   Of high Olympus utter'd slavish sighs.
> When from the Heavens I saw her first descend,
>   My heart took fire, and only burning pains,

> They were my pleasures – they my Life's sad end;
> Love pour'd her beauty into my warm veins.
>
> (*Letters*, pp. 217-18)

Like the Dante sonnet, this also lifts up at line 9; and line 12, quoted singly to Dilke the day before, outdoes the rest by far. Ronsard has: 'Amour coula ses beautez en mes veines'; Keats adds 'warm', so that unavoidably we must apprehend the incoming of love and beauty as a cold shock. The fire, the burning, in line 10 also have no basis in the French. We may call them conventionally Petrarchan – love is an icy fire – but Keats is doing what he characteristically does: converting the conventional into the true voice of feeling, saying the life, the closeness of love and death, as it truly is. He is already approaching next April's images of Cantos V and VI and 'La Belle Dame Sans Merci'.

Keats called the translation free, and having copied it out for Reynolds he casually admitted: 'I had not the original by me when I wrote it, and did not recollect the purport of the last lines – ' Few people attempt a translation without constantly and anxiously referring to the original there in front of them. Here, for reference after the event, is that original:

> Nature ornant Cassandre qui devoyt
>   De sa douceur forcer les plus rebelles,
>   La composa de cent beautez nouvelles
>   Que dès mille ans en espargne elle avoyt.
> De tous les biens qu'Amour-oiseau couvoit
>   Au plus beau ciel cherement sous ses ailes,
>   Elle enrichit les graces immortelles
>   De son bel oeil, qui les Dieux emouvoyt.
> Du ciel a peine elle etoyt descendue,
>   Quand je la vi, quand mon ame esperdue
>   En devint folle, et d'un si poignant trait,
> Amour coula ses beautez en mes veines,
>   Qu'autres plaisirs je ne sens que mes peines,
>   Ny autre bien qu'adorer son pourtrait.

Ronsard divides his sonnet 4 + 4 + 2 + 4 (a rhyming couplet at lines 9-10); but it is printed as though the arrangement were 4 + 4 + 4 + 2. Keats writes three quatrains, and in each contains the portion of narrative and the essence of the imagery as they are disposed in each four-line block in Ronsard's poem. Thus ll. 1-4: Nature adorns Cassandra; ll. 5-8: Love, like a mother bird, shelters and nurtures her until her beauty is such that it profoundly affects the gods; ll. 9-12: Cassandra comes down from the skies and affects the poet even more profoundly. Retaining that structure, Keats several times follows his own mind. For example, he at once locates Cassandra in the skies, but keeps her there preparing for a thousand years (Ronsard says Nature had been storing the beauties for that long); he adds shadow to the wings of Love and turns the gods into *cloudy* kings. All the brighter then, all the more overwhelming, is Cassandra's epiphany in the final quatrain; by which time Keats, still adhering to the structure, has come into his voice and certainly has no need of Ronsard's final two lines, the purport of which he says he could not recollect.

This is an odd way to translate a poem. To describe it I will recall what Keats said about Tom in the letter to Dilke: 'his identity presses upon me'. Ronsard's sonnet, read and enjoyed, even absent presses its identity upon him. He translates it, asserting his own identity against it as he does so. Cary's Dante affected him similarly: he dreamed on it, composed on it, directed its images into the expression of his own life. Keats knew himself to be profoundly susceptible to the identities of other people. In a room full of people he was, he said, annihilated. He made an active virtue of what actually and inevitably happened to him, understanding annihilation of the self as a necessary factor in being a poet. Here he is in Scotland, approaching Burns's cottage: 'One of the pleasantest means of annulling self is approaching such a shrine...' (*Letters*, p. 175). Identity is too large a subject for now, but occasional thoughts on it will help understand the workings of translation, and not just in the case of Keats. The foreign author, the foreign language, presses upon the translator who will react more or less self-assertively in the encounter. Keats was quite peculiarly gifted in the two movements of that vital dialectic: dangerously open to other identities, passionately assertive of his own. We can stay with him, and with Ronsard, a while longer in this discussion.

A year later, 21 September 1819, in three letters he was writing on that same day, one to Woodhouse, another to Reynolds, another to George and Georgiana, Keats turned his dealings with foreign languages more definitely towards his own ends.

Again Ronsard was involved. Keats wrote to Woodhouse (from whom he had borrowed the poems the year before): 'I had begun a Sonnet in french of Ronsard – on my word 'tis verry capable of poetry...I intended to call it La Platonique Chevalresque – I like the second line – Non ne suis si audace a languire / De m'empresser au coeur vos tendres mains. &c' That is, he attempts a sonnet of his own in a French like Ronsard's; which cancels out his earlier thorough disparagement of the French language; and, more importantly, makes a part of his meditation at this time on the nature of, and how to achieve, his own true vernacular. For in the letter to Woodhouse this passage concerning Ronsard's French abruptly interrupts a substantial quotation from *The Fall of Hyperion*; to which, just as abruptly, Keats then returns, saying: 'Here is what I had written for a sort of induction...', copying out lines 1-11 of that poem (*Letters*, pp. 388-89). This sudden juxtapostion, which may seem accidental or merely wilful in the letter to Woodhouse, looks decidedly meaningful when it is repeated, in its essential components at least (foreign language, the true English vernacular), in the other two letters being written on that day.

In the autumn of 1819, coming ever more confidently into his own voice (he copied out the 'Ode to Autumn', just composed, for Woodhouse), Keats was also benefitting greatly, and in a writerly way, from dealings with literature in a foreign language. In the letter to George and Georgiana he set out the programme of his studies:

> In the course of a few months I shall be as good an Italian Scholar as I am a french one. I am reading Ariosto at present: not managing more than six or eight stanzas at a time. When I have done this language so as to be able to read it tolerably well – I shall set myself to get complete in latin, and there my learning must stop. I do not think of venturing upon Greek. I would not go even so far were I not persuaded of the power the knowledge of any language gives one – the fact is I like to be acquainted with foreign languages.
> (*Letters*, pp. 424-25)

He lists some authors he will have access to when his Latin and his Italian are up to scratch. But adds: 'I shall never become attach'd to a foreign idiom so as to put it into my writings.' And turns at once to Milton:

> The Paradise lost though so fine in itself is a curruption of our Language – it should be kept as it is unique – a curiosity – a beautiful and grand Curiosity. The most remarkable Production of the world. A northern dialect accommodating itself to greek and latin inversions and intonations. The purest english I think – or what ought to be the purest – is Chatterton's. The Language had existed long enough to be entirely uncorrupted of Chaucer's gallicisms, and still the old words are used. Chatterton's language is entirely northern. I prefer the native music of it to Milton's cut by feet. I have but lately stood on my guard against Milton. Life to him would be death to me. Miltonic verse cannot be written but in the vein of art – I wish to devote myself to another sensation –

Milton, he thinks, is a writer who became so attached to a foreign idiom as to put it into his writings. And the question for Keats – we need all three letters together to see it clearly – is, on a general level, that of a national literature's truest language; and, on the particular, the language of his own poem *The Fall of Hyperion*. He quotes extensively from *Hyperion* to Woodhouse, making an abrupt excursion into Ronsard's French whilst doing so; and to George and Georgiana he expounds on the value of learning foreign languages, but shifts then into concern for pure English. It is in the letter to Reynolds that he makes a test case of himself. He writes:

> I always somehow associate Chatterton with autumn. He is the purest writer in the English Language. He has no French idiom, or particles like Chaucer – 'tis genuine English Idiom in English Words. I have given up Hyperion – there were too many Miltonic inversions in it – Miltonic verse can not be written but in an artful or rather artist's humour. I wish to give myself up to other sensations. English ought to be kept up. It may be interesting to you to pick out some lines from Hyperion and put a mark X to the false beauty proceeding from art, and one || to the true voice of feeling. Upon my soul 'twas imagination I cannot make the distinction – Every now & then there is a Miltonic intonation – But I cannot make the division properly.
>
> (*Letters*, pp. 384-85)

Though Keats may not be able to make the distinction in practice, he does nonetheless feel that a diction may be false or true, and he is listening out for the one and the other. Milton's language tends to the false, Chatterton's to the true. Milton corrupts his language, 'a northern dialect', by 'accommodating [it] to greek and latin inversions and intonations'. Chatterton, 'the marvellous Boy', who killed himself in 1770 at the age of seventeen, arrived at a language which Keats, contrasting it with Milton's, could declare to be pure, by travelling back three hundred years into the foreign country of the past and writing in the voice of Thomas Rowley, priest. My interest here is not in the viability of Keats's distinctions, nor in the justice of his verdicts on those authors, but only in his striving for a true vernacular (the nation's, his own); in his considering English in the light of foreignness; and in his more or less explicitly entertaining the idea that one might better understand one's own language, and even come into the proper use of it, through dealings with 'abroad'.

In older poetics the would-be poet was commonly told he must study foreign languages and translate from them if he wished to master his own. Martin Opitz, in his *Buch von der Deutschen Poeterey* (1624), cited in support of this injunction the example of Ronsard who spent a good twelve years working at Greek texts, 'the better to knead and manipulate his native French'. In less time (he had less) but with near-manic intensity Hölderlin steeped himself in Greek, for the good of his German. In 1794, before he had done much translating himself, he made these remarks on the subject to a friend then translating Virgil: 'The great Roman's spirit will surely be a wonderful strengthener of your own. In the struggle with his language yours must become more and more agile and vigorous.' And later: 'You are right. Translation does our language good, like gymnastics. It gets beautifully supple when forced to accommodate itself thus to foreign beauty and greatness and also often to foreign whims.' Then he added this qualification or anxiety: 'Language is the organ of our intellect and feelings, the sign of our ideas; we are the ones it has to obey. If it serves too long abroad there's a danger, I think, that it won't ever again do what we want it to do: be the free and pure and one and only appropriate expression of the spirit within.' Translation is like service abroad; the poet goes abroad, like a journeyman, to learn his craft. That way, through the foreign, he comes into what is properly his; but risks losing himself, so doing. In December 1801, having by then done a good deal of translation and written many poems, Hölderlin commented 'our own has to be learned just as much as the foreign...because...the free use of our own is the hardest thing'. His translation of Pindar's Olympian and Pythian Odes in the spring and summer of 1800 is an extreme example of a writer's learning through the foreign what will be most peculiarly his own. Hölderlin translated some six thousand lines of the notoriously difficult Pindar, and, so it seems, only for his own benefit, with no thought of publication. He translated him literally, line by line, cleaving as close as possible to the Greek, retaining the word order, going for the most concrete and literal sense, breaking the lines drastically as they were broken in Greek in the edition he was using. The result was a thing neither Greek not German, a text for most of its way not intelligible without the original, but now and then – and this was the looked-for outcome and reward – surfacing by that entirely mechanical means into something wonderfully beautiful, strange and just within the borders of native intelligibility, and seeming to hindsight like the ghost, still wanting substance, of Hölderlin's own late language. Using the terms I have borrowed and applied from Keats, we may say that Hölderlin allowed the identity of Pindar's Greek to press upon him almost to the point of his own annihilation; but came through the ordeal, into his own vernacular, by an equal act of self-assertion.

That dialectic of native and foreign in the individual writer is at work also in the national language itself. A great writer, like Milton or Hölderlin, contributes materially to the dialectic on the national level. Keats objected to Milton's latinate English, calling it 'a curruption of our Language'. He felt Milton was having a bad influence on him; hankered after something more purely English (castigating even Chaucer for gallicisms); and located that purity in the forger or ventriloquist Chatterton. Keats seems close, there at least (see especially the letter to Reynolds), to equating 'the true voice of feeling' with an English not marked by any foreign tongue. But some foreignness may be good for both the individual writer and the language of the nation. The whole effort of poetry is to make us realise things, very often things we know already but, because of familiarity, have lost the feeling for. Poetry revives the feeling, very often by an act of rendering strange. A syntax and an idiom marked by the writer's 'service abroad' *may* work in that way. The question, in translations and in original compositions, will be how much foreignness can the native language take, before it loses its own identity. Hölderlin's Pindar, not intended for any reader but himself, does incur such a loss; but his Sophocles translations, which he published, are *effectively* strange, the German is haunted by the Greek and is induced to do things far beyond its usual frontiers. Hölderlin's own language, unmistakably his own, the true voice of his own feeling, still carrries in its bloodstream that haunting by the Greek, and is strange, works estrangingly, troubles and disorientates us like a language of elsewhere. But in saying that, I am not saying very much. Hölderlin may be an extreme example, but in practice, when it works, all poetic language, however demotic and up-to-the minute its mode, departs in some wise from the norm, affects us with strangeness, and may indeed sound like a language of translation. Graves called the poet an 'ambassador of Otherwhere', and a foreign accent, more or less pronounced, perhaps comes with the job.

Identity is not a stable thing. It may alter, suffer diminution, even be extinguished, precisely under foreign influence. But the individual and the national culture have to be open to what is foreign to them, and run the risk. Standstill and hedging around are not an option. Best would be an essential identity that, always open and running through numerous metamorphoses, asserts itself and thrives. Goethe is often cited as an outstanding example of such continuity in continual change. His sense of self-identity, his essential confidence in it, was vast; but the German culture that he, as German writer, represents, has rarely been so sure of itself. Compared with the literatures of England or France, that of Germany is a thing of fits and starts. This may be largely due to the amorphousness and instability (until quite recent times) of the nation itself; but the phenomenon is of interest here, more than its causes. During the first half of the seventeenth century, when German-speaking lands were the chief battlefield in the Thirty Years War, German culture, indeed the very language, was subjected to an adulteration so severe as to be almost fatal. English, French, Spanish, Italian, Polish, Croatian, Swedish came with the armies over the native tongue, and it was in that context that Martin Opitz, in his already mentioned *Buch von der Deutschen Poetery*, sought to affirm or actually to establish a national literature. But when he wanted to present specimens in the vernacular of the genres and forms he was describing, largely he had to supply these himself, by translation from abroad. To demonstrate the sonnet, for example, he offers his own translations of Ronsard. German literature in the seventeenth century was brought into being *by main force of translation*. In the latter half of the eighteenth century, it had to be revived again, pulled up by its bootstraps, when French threatened to overwhelm it wholly. To counter that French, German writers turned to English. The anxiety of influence has always been particularly keen in Germany.

English is a self-confident literature. Still, like the literatures of other European countries, it had to understand, define and assert itself in the Renaissance. It did so much later than Italian, much earlier than German. Sir Philip Sidney, in his *Apologie for Poetrie* (written 1580/81) laments, just as Opitz will, the poor state of the art in his native land, and advises on how it may be improved. Much of that advice has to do with how the vernacular language actually works, what its demands and possibilities are. This self-reflection was necessary in an age whose writers were schooled in Latin and inclined to think that dead language superior to their living native tongue. Thus Sidney has to rule in the matter of scansion, distinguishing the English procedure from that of Latin and Greek: 'though wee doe not observe quantity, yet wee observe the accent very precisely', and glancing also at the ways of French, Italian, Spanish and Dutch. English, essentially sure of itself, imported and adapted vigorously, and translation was the chief means. Chapman, wanting to English Homer and needing an equivalent for the Greek hexameter, first, in the *Iliad* (1598-1611), tried the fourteen-syllable iambic line, rhyming mostly, but not always, with the next; then, for the *Odyssey* (1614-15), shifted to pentameters, rhyming in couplets. There are advantages and disadvantages in each; the important thing here is to recognise that each is a choice, a strategy, an effort at equivalent effect in the native tongue. When the Earl of Surrey set himself to translate Books II and IV of Virgil's *Aeneid*, his invention to render the Latin hexameter was the unrhyming iambic pentameter, blank verse; a line which soon established itself pre-eminently in English drama. Thus translation enlarged the possibilities of the vernacular. Surrey and Sir Thomas Wyatt both did translations of sonnets by Petrarch, Surrey changing the Italian arrangement (two quatrains, two tercets) into the English (three quatrains and a concluding couplet) taken on by Shakespeare. Wyatt's versions are earlier and they, and indeed many of his own poems, were felt to be metrically irregular by his first editor Tottel (in 1557) who straightened them out. Certainly they were rougher than Surrey's. For example, their translations of Petrach's 'Amor, che nel penser mio vive et regna...':

WYATT:
The longe love, that in my thought doeth harbar
And in myn hert doeth kepe his residence
Into my face preseth with bold pretence,
And therin campeth, spreding his baner.
She that me lerneth to love and suffre
And will that my trust, and lustes negligence
Be rayned by reason, shame, and reverence
With his hardines taketh displeasure.
Wherwithall, unto the hertes forrest he fleith,
Leving his entreprise with payne and cry
And there him hideth and not appereth.
What may I do when my maister fereth,
But, in the felde, with him to lyve and dye?
For goode is the liff, ending faithfully.

SURREY:
Love that liveth and reigneth in my thought,
That built its seat within my captive breast,
Clad in the arms wherein with me he fought,
Oft in my face he doth his banner rest.
But she that taught me love, and suffer pain,
My doubtful hope and eke my hot desire
With shamefast cloak to shadow and refrain,
Her smiling grace converteth straight to ire.
And coward Love then to the heart apace
Taketh his flight, where he doth lurk and plain
His purpose lost, and dare not show his face.
For my lord's guilt thus faultless bide I pain.
Yet from my lord shall not my foot remove:
Sweet is his death that takes his end by love.

Wyatt seems to be harking back to the rhythms of older alliterative verse, Surrey to be establishing the normative iambic pentameter. At which point we rejoin Keats and his preference for 'the native music' of Chatterton's pretended fifteenth-century poems to Milton's 'cut by feet', and his delighted shock at hearing Homer in Chapman's 'rough-hewn' English. After too much Pope and Milton, and feeling that this own verse was wandering away from true, he wished to give himself up to 'other sensations'. ('I wish to devote myself to another sensation', *Letters*, p. 425.) The rougher seems truer. 'Sensation' is the apt word there. He had written to his publisher Hessey in October 1818: 'The Genius of Poetry must work out its own salvation in a man: It cannot be matured by law and precept, but by sensation & watchfulness in itself' (*Letters*, pp. 222-23). That was exactly his stance, one of 'sensation & watchfulness', in listening to varieties of English, to hear his own.

How far should a translator domesticate the foreign original? This is a question that translators, or at least writers about translation, are forever posing. Since my chief concern here is the language of poetry, which should, as I have said, always carry with it some feeling of 'coming from abroad', the way of thorough domestication seems to me the wrong one. The journey abroad, figuratively and literally, is essential, and I do think some mark of it should adhere, to work defamilarisingly on things we think we know. I began with Keats, and made an icon of his encounter with Homer through the good offices of a translator and a friend; and I shall end with him too, as he looked after his one literal return from abroad, in the late summer of 1818, when he finished his trek through Scotland at Inverness, took a smack from Cromarty and after ten days at sea, docked at London Bridge. He hurried at once to see his Hampstead friends. Does Scotland count as abroad? Perhaps I shall be allowed it; literally, for Keats's own observation 'I am for the first time in a country where a foreign Language is spoken – they gabble away Gaelic at a vast rate' (*Letters*, p. 189); figuratively, for the spirit in which he set off. He wrote (already well into it):

> I should not have consented to myself these four Months tramping in the highlands but that I thought it would give me more experience, rub off more Prejudice, use me to more hardship, identify finer scenes load me with grander Mountains, and strengthen more my reach in Poetry, than would stopping at home among Books even though I should reach Homer. (*Letters*, p. 193)

The very proper Mrs Dilke describes his re-appearance from abroad: 'John Keats arrived here last night, as brown and as shabby as you can imagine; scarcely any shoes left, his jacket all torn at the back, a fur cap, a great plaid, and his knapsack. I cannot tell what he looked like' (*Letters*, p. 212).

For every reader some such shock of foreignness is salutary, and poetry has the power to issue it. And for the nation, especially if that nation is English-speaking, the continual shock of the foreign is absolutely indispensable. Too much, too speedy, a domestication is a form of annexation, one-sided, there is no dialectic in it, no give and take. We need the foreignness of the other country; and also, just as important, the foreignness of the past. 'The past is another country. They do things differently there.' The assumption that everyone was or is just like us, or jolly well ought to be, is very stupid, and might, if sustained much longer, be fatal.

SOURCES:

Keats's letters are referred to in *The Letters of John Keats*, edited by Maurice Buxton Forman, third edition (OUP, 1947); his poems either in the *Letters* or in Keats, *The Complete Poems*, edited by Miriam Allott (Longman, 1970). Other works cited or referred to are Robert Gittings, *John Keats* (Pelican Books, 1971), and my own *Hölderlin* (OUP, 1988).

Use and Ornament

Renaissance and seventeenth-century handbooks of poetics largely adopted the format and the terminology of handbooks of rhetoric. The whole business of composition was set out under two large captions, *res* and *verba*, which denoted its phases: first think of a subject (*res*) then consider what words (*verba*) to clothe that subject in. Under *inventio* advice was given on where to find the material and the illustrative instances that might make your poem more effective. The qualities its language should have – purity, clarity, decorative colouring (*ornatus*) – were discussed under *elocutio*. Users of such handbooks were routinely reminded that poets, unlike rhetoricians, are born, not made; but a rapprochement, if not quite a fusing, of the two disciplines was acceptable until the latter half of the eighteenth century, when much Romantic theory and practice insisted on a separation. Novalis, for example, thought poetry a quite peculiar thing; it was itself, and an end in itself; it and rhetoric were poles apart. One point of contention was whether poetry could be made to serve an end, have a utilitarian purpose, in the way that rhetoric – a necessary art for barristers and politicians – obviously and rightly could. Keats declared: 'We hate poetry that has a palpable design upon us – and if we do not agree, seems to put its hand in its breeches pocket' (*Letters*, p. 96). Now, barristers and politicians may have no need of poetry, but poets cannot dispense with rhetoric, and that is not a cause for shame or regret. The question whether poetry can be effective – whether it can persuade, change opinion, make things happen – will always want an answer, especially when the times are very pressing and when poets feel compelled by their bad consciences to intervene. It is easy then, as the world marches on to catastrophe just the same, to conclude that 'poetry makes nothing happen', and cannot prevent things from happening either.

Brecht is an exemplary writer in this context. In the late 1920s, after his early years of anarchic individualism, he committed himself to marxism and to communism, and wrote for that cause. The times made such a commitment likely – many of his friends did the same – and also for reasons in his own psychology and for his further artistic development he needed discipline, purpose, belief and direction. Though known (still) primarily as a man of the theatre, he was also, and even more abundantly, a lyric poet. Theatre – some strands of it, at least – has a long tradition of being morally instructive; it has regularly served that end. The difficulties arrive with the shift of genre, the poem, if we agree with Keats, being not the place for any such 'palpable design'. Brecht is a good example because he would not think of his lyric poetry as a zone apart; he wanted to use it for the cause, wanted it to be as useful as the theatre was. He reconnects, beyond the Romantic interruption, with the older tradition in which poetry and rhetoric were at least on speaking terms.

In 1927 Brecht adjudicated a poetry competition but refused to award the prize because, he said, none of the five hundred submissions were 'of any proper use'. And he added: 'lyric poetry especially ought without doubt to be a thing we must be able to examine for its usefulness'. By 'especially' he was perhaps implying that lyric poetry looked very much like a thing a modern age could well do without. In the previous year he had written a poem, 'Coals for Mike', which celebrates a concretely useful act. Every night the comrades of a dead brakeman fling a lump of coal from their locomotive into his widow's garden as they pass. He died because of the conditions on the Wheeling Railroad. His comrades pay his widow a sort of pension, in coal, out of the company's stock. The last stanza reads:

> This poem is dedicated to the comrades
> Of the brakeman Mike McCoy
> (Who died because his lungs were too weak
> On the coal trains of Ohio)
> For comradeship.

There at the very outset of his thirty years of commitment to the cause Brecht set an icon of usefulness. Would that the poem might be as manifestly and immediately useful as the lump of coal! Instead – it is a matter of spheres of activity, akin to the question of genre within the sphere of writing – the best he can do, and it is no small thing, is memorialise the act and offer the poem as reciprocation for the coal.

Brecht gave a lot of thought to the nature, shape and function of lyric poetry in 'the dark times', which were his own. He addressed quite particularly the question of how he, as a poet, could serve the cause he believed in. How should he fit his poetry for the struggle? After Hitler's seizure of power in January 1933, he went into exile (he would have been killed had he not) and fought fascism from there, with the weapons at his disposal, the spoken, broadcast and written word. Exile – in Denmark, Finland, the Soviet Union, America – lessened his effectiveness. The premise, the very ground of being useful, was to write in accordance with reality; and the writer in exile easily gets things wrong. Also, his marxist analysis of National Socialism was inadequate in several respects, and where that analysis shapes the poems, it harms them. (No amount of 'poetry' will make wrong ideas right.) Much of this difficulty and likelihood of failure he himself anticipated, and factored it into the writing of the poems. Hence – surprising to those who think him dogmatic – the tentative and enquiring gesture of many of the poems.

The poet who wishes to be useful has to be informed, and Brecht did his best to be. Next, in his view, the poems themselves, in their subjects and in their workings, must accord with the reality their writer has observed. In an essay of 1938 entitled 'Unrhyming Verse in Irregular Rhythms' Brecht set out the poetics which, so he believed, the times and his responsibility in them necessitated. The essay articulated what had been his practice for some years. The essence of the poetics is an almost classical notion of consonance, fittingness, decorum. The times are violent, full of struggle, discord and contradiction. The lines of verse must be consonant with that fact. There must be no 'formal neutralising' of discordant subjects; rhyme, suggestive of harmony and by its euphonious repetition inclining a reader to sleepy acquiescence, must be eschewed. The verse must be wakeful, nervous, agile, testing.

Objections can be made to this simple theory of consonance, and Brecht himself ignored it whenever he saw advantage in doing so. But I want for my argument here the idea that the usefulness of a poem will be enhanced not only by a sound grasp of the realities it addresses but also by a formal consonance with those realities.

Reading through his *Svendborg Poems* (1938) and comparing them with his earlier work, Brecht noted that 'from a bourgeois point of view...an astonishing impoverishment [had] taken place'. He meant not only the willed avoidance of euphony and harmony mentioned above, but also the deliberate exclusion of traditional lyric subjects such as love and nature. In this too – the choice of subjects – he was aiming at consonance. Capitalism, he argued, and its (to the marxist) natural development, fascism, had laid waste the landscape in which the lyric poet lives and writes. Again and again he would concede that the struggle, in which they had no choice but to engage, deformed and dehumanised the strugglers; it reduced and impoverished them. The poetry had to match that impoverishment. The poem 'To Those Born Later' admits and laments the harm done to all who are engaged in the necessary fight for more humane conditions:

> Hatred, even of baseness
> Contorts the features.
> Anger, even against injustice
> Makes the voice hoarse.
> Oh we who wanted to prepare the ground
> For friendliness
> Could not ourselves be friendly.

And 'Bad Times for Lyric Poetry' laments a like impoverishment in the poem.

> I do not see
> The green boats and the cheerful sails in the sound.
> All I see
> Are the torn nets of the fishermen.
> Why do I make it my only subject
> That the women of the village, at forty, walk with a stoop?
> The girls' breasts
> Are as warm as ever.

> In my poetry a rhyme
> Would seen to be almost an insolence.

> There is a quarrel in me
> Between my delight in the apple tree in bloom
> And my horror at the housepainter's speeches.

But only the latter
Drives me to my desk.

('The housepainter' is Hitler. We might note that the poem, mentioning him, does actually celebrate the things it forbids itself.)

Both the above poems follow Brecht's (and Lenin's) chilling dictum: 'We derive our aesthetics, like our ethics, from the needs of our struggle.' Making oneself useful in the dark times, as citizen or as poet, making oneself fit for the task, entails a reduction in humanity. This they knew, regretted, and accepted.

Brecht's 'German Satires' are a good example of verses fitted for a particular use. They were written, as anti-fascist propaganda, to be broadcast on the Free German Radio, first from Spain and then, after Franco's victory, from the Baltic. That medium was subject to frequent interference by the enemy the poems were directed against. Having a clear objective and knowing the conditions in which he must operate, Brecht devised verses capable of having at least some effect even if they were interrupted and fragmented. The polemical units were small, his lineation worked for the survival of the satire and the message. Thus the poem 'The Cares of the Chancellor' is composed of six autonomous units. The fourth reads:

Neighbouring countries
Speak of our country only with contempt.
Aloud they condemn
The mismanagement and the violence.
Often, so it is said,
When the Chancellor reads foreign newspapers
He weeps.
Then the Minister for Propaganda urges the people
To dry their Chancellor's tears.

This is a poetics of particular function, in particular time and place. The poems themselves are excellent of their kind, but are not much read now for the obvious reason that, tied to particularities, they lapse with them. And needless to say, though they add to the stock of revulsion against fascism, they did not stop it doing its worst.

'Coals for Mike' memorialises an act of solidarity. After that date, Brecht repeatedly used his poetry to give proper due to people who, because of their class, had not received it. The poem 'Questions of a Worker who Reads' announces the shift of interest; history is defamiliarised; light thrown on its real makers.

> Young Alexander conquered India.
> All on his own?
> Caesar defeated the Gauls.
> Did he not even have a cook with him?
> Philip of Spain wept when his fleet
> Went down. Was he the only one
> Who wept?

That poem is programmatic, others carry the programme out; and in the best of them the particular instance is treated in such a way that its wider applicability is released. In brief, the deed or persons worthy of being remembered become, with no loss of particularity, figurative. Brecht heard of a village of carpet weavers in Turkestan who, having donated money they could ill afford for a plaster bust in honour of Lenin, decided to spend the money on petrol instead, to kill the malarial mosquitoes infesting their swampy locality. Like the brakemen, they do something concretely useful. In his poem 'The Carpet Weavers of Kuyan-Bulak honour Lenin' Brecht honours them for doing so and for, in his view, correctly understanding Lenin's teaching. Generalise that, and the 'moral' is the lively and humane one that you should apply what you have learned to the particular circumstances you actually have to live in. You best honour your teacher by doing so. Soon, that way, pupil may be released from teacher.

That poem does what good poems have always done: it exceeds the immediate occasion, being apt to it (useful to it?), but surviving, which means continuing to work, beyond it. Brecht did not do this in the 'German Satires', and did not even try to; he was willing there to work for the moment and lapse with it. But I am edging this discussion now towards the view that poetry, even one as engaged in the moment as Brecht's, works better, is more (lastingly) effective, the more it obeys its own peculiar calling and works towards its own characteristic ends – one of which is to generalise, to evade death by making lasting images.

Here are a couple of poems from Brecht's 'A German War Primer'. We may use them to consider the question: How do Brecht's poems actually work?

> On the wall was written in chalk:
> They want a war.
> The man who wrote it
> Has already fallen.
>
> * * *
>
> General, man is very useful
> He can fly and he can kill.
> But he has one defect:
> He can think.
>
> * * *
>
> The housepainter speaks of great times to come.
> The woods still grow.
> The fields still bear.
> The cities still stand
> The people still breathe.

They quicken the intelligence and the moral sense. They excite grief and outrage. The strengthen the spirit of contradiction. The lineation itself alerts us.

'Beds for the Night' has an unsettling structure. It will not allow the reader's mind to rest assured:

> I hear that in New York
> On the corner of 26th Street and Broadway
> A man stands every evening in the winter months
> And begging passers-by
> Gets a bed for the night for the homeless gathered there.
> The world is not changed by this
> Relations between human beings are not improved
> The age of exploitation is not made any shorter.
> But a few men have a bed for the night
> For one night long they are out of the wind
> The snow that was meant for them falls on the streets.
>
> You reading this, do not put down the book.
> A few men have a bed for the night
> For one night long they are out of the wind
> The snow that was meant for them falls on the streets.
> But the world is not changed by this
> Relations between human beings are not improved
> The age of exploitation is not made any shorter.

Brecht does have a view, and seeks to persuade his readers to embrace it. In plays, poems and essays he does have a palpable design on us. In 'Beds for the Night' he is advancing the opinion that individual acts of charity acts don't help the large situation, which is systematic exploitation and oppression. Indeed, by palliating, they prolong it, and in that sense are actually harmful. But the structure: 'You are sure of that, your feelings are very definite: Now consider this' – that structure, in itself, as the structure of a challenge put to the heart and the mind, exceeds, and may even induce a reader to contradict, the author's known and immediate intention. Brecht's poems excite a state of mind which might actually resist any particular directive. Primarily they quicken the sceptical intelligence, and scepticism, like freedom, is not divisible. Two of his most memorable poems, 'The Doubter' and 'In Praise of Doubt' actually 'teach' scepticism. Even towards one's teacher. Brecht's own gloss on I Corinthians 13.2 was that it was not faith [in German: 'der Glaube'] but disbelief [in German: 'der Unglaube'] that moves mountains. True, in the service of his own ideology he wished to inculcate disbelief only as a preliminary stage, to cure you of false views before inducing you into the true ones. But once taught to disbelieve, the good pupil is not so easily reined in.

Brecht is a great poet, one of the three or four best in the whole of German literature, and it should not surprise us to see him, so to speak, outwitted, exceeded and contradicted by his own poems. It is perhaps often the case that the poem is more various than its author, in his or her life as a citizen, has power or inclination to be. Brecht thought and wrote dialectically; which is to say, he made progress through 'contraries'. Being himself the very spirit of contradiciton, he not only invited and required contradiction from his readers and interlocutors, he invited and required it, towards himself, from his own poems. This *poète engagé*, a determined user of his writing for definite political ends, is also, paradoxically, an implicit and sometimes explicit advocate for the autonomy of the lyric poem. His practice allowed the poem to be its own peculiar and contradictory self, to work as it was meant to, as a poem. And more than once, though perfectly well aware of the direction – into 'impoverishment', harsh consonance, political tendentiousness – he himself had taken, he conceded the effectiveness (usefulness) in particular circumstances of poetry quite unlike his own.

In 1940, by then in Finland, Brecht was dipping into Matthew

Arnold's anthology of Wordsworth's poems and lit on 'She was a phantom of delight...' It prompted him to reflect on the very varied effectiveness of lyric verse. Hitler seemed unstoppable, Britain, the last hope, looked about to be invaded. It occurred to Brecht that such a poem, innocent of all political point and easily dismissed by critics like himself as 'petty-bourgeois', might well, in those terrible times, have a good effect. He noted 'precisely in this inhuman situation "a lovely apparition, sent / to be a moment's ornament" may awaken a memory of situations more worthy of human beings'. In Heaney's terms, it might – by very virtue of being an autonomous poem – effect some redress. Two years later, by then in Hollywood, Brecht noted in his journal that writing even politically committed poetry there seemed finnicky, pointless, an occupation in an ivory tower; but concluded the note with this enigmatic but, I think, determinedly hopeful sentence: 'Such poetry is a message in a bottle, the battle for Smolensk is also a battle for lyric poetry.' Poetry, launched in the dark times in the faint hope of beaching where it might be of some encouragement, is a small equivalent of the battle being fought by the Russian people against Hitler for their homeland. That is why the two statements are set side by side in one sentence. But the latter half also means that the Russian people are fighting for the survival of humane life altogether; and without humane life poetry itself cannot survive. It does survive in the struggle, when there is still the possibility of conditions 'more worthy of human beings'; but the total victory of fascism (they were fighting a total war) would exterminate it in the extermination of the humane life of the people.

Dissident writers under a dictatorship may properly complain that their very dissidence is dictated to them. East German writers used to speak of 'die aufgezwungenen Themen' – the subjects forced upon them. They were bound by the cruel dialectic of state and dissident, unfree, always dictated to, always merely *in reaction*. Their verse had to be 'political'. That at least was the obvious reaction, and the obvious form of resistance. But another strategy, practised in China by poets like Bei Dao, was to write 'apolitical' verse – verse whose subjective stance and whose topics (love, nature, the individual self) belonged to older traditions of the lyric. In context, that was a highly political and dissident thing to do, and they were persecuted accordingly, for their 'bourgeois individualism'. Seamus Heaney in Northern Ireland clearly felt that his subjects were being 'forced on him', and escaped into a writing where he would be freer to allow the poem, political or not, to effect its own resistance and redress. Brecht in the struggle against Hitler, writers in the East throughout the Cold War, Heaney in the Troubles all felt more or less dictated to in the subject and the mode of their lyric writing; and the strategies they adopted for the survival of their poetry are well worth studying. All, one way or another, rightly steer towards an insistence on the autonomy of the lyric.

The poetic word always seems to matter more under oppression and threat. Their fellow-citizens look to the poets to be of present help. The grave and dangerous responsibilities that poets under a dictatorship have to bear do at least bring with them a corroboration of the value of their efforts. Much less, if any, such corroboration is forthcoming in Britain. Poets in Britain are free to write more or less what they like, chiefly because no one in power cares tuppence what they write. This freedom, certainly a great benefit, does carry with it the risk of pointlessness and irresponsibility. Some poets, from certain groups in British society, may indeed feel there are issues so urgent they have no option but to address them, almost to the exclusion of all others. They may indeed feel their subjects are 'forced upon them'. But many, perhaps most, don't feel that, and they risk slipping into the limbo of personal malaise and language games. Dictated to them or not, there is in fact a large and various social obligation on poets writing in Briain today. Day in day out, the language of our managers and leaders cries out to be contradicted. Poetry is peculiarly good at contradicting. The exact shape and practice of the contradiction will have to be devised in every new case, by every poet again and again. Agility is necessary.

Thinking about Wordsworth's poem Brecht noted 'Art *is* an autonomous zone, though never under any circumstances autarkic.' That is, though never a zone apart, never self-sufficient, never a thing independent of and untouched by external political reality, the lyric poem does operate according to laws which are all its own. It has a proper autonomy, and will be most effective in its dealings with and opposition to the state when it abides by and insists on that autonomy. Clearly, all this is very vexed. Insisting on its autonomy, the lyric risks losing its hold on the realities in which it does and must exist, it risks losing its power to matter. But that is only a risk, and there are risks in all the undertakings that do matter. Seamus Heaney worked at defining the poem's ability 'to answer back' in his Oxford Lectures, and I don't need to go over the same ground here. The gist is, the poem will do best, will actually benefit us as citizens best, if it insists on its peculiar mode. When a poem works, then by means peculiar to it, by rhyme, by a pleasing arrangement, by its clarity and *ornatus*, we are enlivened, quickened in our humanity, made more alert to more possibilities. And a human being awkened like that is a better citizen, and more likely to resist the reduction of his or her humanity being practised more or less systematically by the state. The poem comes with beauty and gives pleasure. Brecht himself, having willed his own impoverishment, readily conceded that in analysing the peculiar value and effects of a poem we cannot dispense with the concept of beauty and need not be ashamed of it either. His poems are beautiful, their 'impoverishment' (whatever it meant in the humanity of their author) is really a pleasing fitness for the task.

Now I must go back to Keats, and connect his dislike of poems that have a palpable design on us with his thesis that the quality which goes to form 'a Man of Achievement, especially in Literature' is '*Negative Capability*'. Typically, he had this insight during a conversation, or to be more precise, using his own words, during 'not a dispute but a disquisition' in December 1817 when, as he says, 'several things dove-tailed' in his mind (*Letters*, p. 72). The other party to this disquisition was Charles Wentworth Dilke and it may be that Keats's sudden realisation came as much from Dilke's own manner or character on that occasion as from the matter in hand. Further along in their friendship Keats summed him up as one 'who cannot feel he has a personal identity unless he has made up his Mind about every thing'. Whereas, in Keats's own view, 'the only means of strengthening one's intellect is to make up ones mind about nothing – to let the mind be a thoroughfare for all thoughts'. Dilke, he goes on, is 'not a select party. The genus is not scarce in the population. All the stubborn arguers you meet with are of the same brood. They never begin upon a subject they have not preresolved on'. In short: 'Dilke will never come at a truth as long as he lives; because he is always trying at it' (*Letters*, p. 426). Keats defined Negative Capability as 'when a man is capable of being in uncertainties, mysteries, doubt, without any irritable reaching after fact and reason'. Dilke was perhaps the immediate example of a person lacking such Capability but Keats actually cites Coleridge who 'would let go by a fine isolated verisimilitude caught from the Penetralium of mystery, from being incapable of remaining content with half-knowledge'. The remarks on Dilke's character and the definition of Negative Capability are of a piece with Keats's frequent scattered assertions that the poet has no character, that he is open to the identities of every thing and every person around him, and that his ability to write resides precisely in this self-annihilating and essentially amoral openness to all possible ways of being human in the world. So that when Keats concludes that the discussion of Negative Capability 'pursued through volumes would perhaps take us no further than this, that with a great poet the sense of Beauty overcomes every other consideration, or rather obliterates all consideration', he is, I think, saying that the requirement of the poem to be itself, to work in its own way, overcomes or obliterates all other consideration, the poem will not be achieved unless the poet manages to suspend judgement and passively attend upon possibilities instead of anxiously seizing on things that may serve as certitudes. Keats disliked poetry that comes at us with a palpable design, just as, thinking of Dilke and his kind, he disliked being argued with by people who 'want to hammer their nail into you and if you turn the point, still they think you wrong'. This subject might indeed be pursued 'through volumes', but all I want from it here is the makings of a contrast with the political commitment and concommitant would-be persuasiveness of poets like Brecht. But I am not making a juxtaposition of opposites, because, as I hope I have shown, in practice Brecht's own poetry, in its structures and actual workings, offers far more suspension, far more negative capability, than his known politics and his statements outside poetry would lead us to expect. A certain degree of negative capability will operate in the writing of any poem, by whatever sort of poet; true poems cannot come about without it. And I might add that they cannot be productively read without it either. A widening of possibilities must take place even if, as in the case of Brecht, his wish as a political persuader was that we should see things his way.

In a letter from Palestine, Keith Douglas defended the new direction his poetry was taking to a friend, J.C. Hall, who thought he had lost his lyricism. Douglas wrote: 'I am surprised you should still expect me to produce musical verse. A lyric form and a lyric approach will do even less good than a journalese approach to the subjects we have to discuss now.' He wrote lyrically, he said, when he was innocent; having 'fallen from grace', which is to say, having seen the war close up, he had to write differently:

> My object (and I don't give a damn about my duty as a poet) is to write true things, significant things in words each one of which works for its place in a line. My rhythms, which you find enervated, are carefully chosen to enable the poems to be *read* as significant speech: I see no reason to be either musical or sonorous about things at present. When I do, I shall be so again, and glad to. I suppose I reflect the cynicism and the careful absence of expectation (it is not quite the same as apathy) with which I view the world.

This note on his poetics concludes:

> To be sentimental or emotional now is dangerous to oneself and to others. To trust anyone or to admit any hope of a better world is criminally foolish, as foolish as it is to stop working for it. It sounds silly to say work without hope, but it can be done.

In all this Douglas resembles Brecht. He devises his poetics to fit his situation and function in the real world. He makes them consonant with it. The hallmark of that consonance is avoidance of 'lyricism', the deliberate disappointing of the traditional expectation of euphony. And there is, as in Brecht, the same acceptance of a diminished humanity (cynicism) forced on him by the times.

Douglas included in this letter (10 August 1943) a first version of his notoriously unemotional and unsentimental poem 'How to Kill'. These lines are the heart of it:

> Now in my dial of glass appears
> the soldier who is going to die.
> He smiles, and moves about in ways

his mother knows, habits of his.
The wires touch his face: I cry
NOW. Death, like a familiar, hears

and look, has made a man of dust
of a man of flesh. This sorcery
I do. Being damned, I am amused
to see the centre of love diffused
and the waves of love travel into vacancy.
How easy it is to make a ghost.

Ted Hughes, introducing Douglas's *Complete Poems*, acknowledged his efforts 'to confront reality undeluded', and said of him that he achieved, at his best, 'convincing authority, distinction, beauty, finality, and even, one feels, practical utility'. Hughes is right about utility: it comes, with beauty, from fitness to the purpose.

Hughes sets Keith Douglas, killed in Normandy, face to face with Wilfred Owen, killed on the Somme. Both quite 'undeluded', they are interestingly different in their treatment of the reality of war. Owen, bearing witness, really did have a palpable design: it was to undelude others and to move them to pity, and in that undertaking he saw no need to suppress pity in himself nor to eschew euphony, pathos and direct appeal:

> If in some smothering dreams you too could pace
> Behind the wagon that we flung him in,
> And watch the white eyes writhing in his face,
> His hanging face, like a devil's sick of sin;
> If you could hear, at every jolt, the blood
> Come gargling from the froth-corrupted lungs,
> Obscene as cancer, bitter as the cud
> Of vile, incurable sores on innocent tongues, –
> My friend, you would not tell with such high zest
> To children ardent for some desperate glory,
> The old Lie: Dulce et decorum est
> Pro patria mori.

Douglas, thinking it dangerous (or just bad art, not effective?) to be emotional or sentimental, wrote quite differently:

> Three weeks gone and the combatants gone
> returning over the nightmare ground
> we found the place again, and found
> the soldier sprawling in the sun.

> The frowning barrel of his gun
> overshadowing. As we came on
> that day, he hit my tank with one
> like the entry of a demon.
>
> Look. Here in the gunpit spoil
> the dishonoured picture of his girl
> who has put: *Steffi. Vergissmeinnicht*
> in a copybook gothic script.
>
> We see him almost with content,
> abased, and seeming to have paid
> and mocked at by his own equipment
> that's hard and good when he's decayed.

And in that withholding of pity, in that openness to the possibility of pitilessness, he is much closer than Owen is to Keats's 'poetical character' which 'has no self – it is every thing and nothing – It has no character – it enjoys light and shade; it lives in gusto, be it foul or fair...' In a word: 'What shocks the virtuous philosopher, delights the cameleon Poet' (*Letters*, pp. 227-28; and see also 67, 69).

In the last two verses of 'Vergissmeinnicht' Douglas shifts perspective to that of the bereaved and in her picture dishonoured girl herself and pity enters, acknowledged as a possibility, through her:

> But she would weep to see today
> how on his skin the swart flies move;
> the dust upon the paper eye
> and the burst stomach like a cave.
>
> For here the lover and killer are mingled
> who had one body and one heart.
> And death who had the soldier singled
> has done the lover mortal hurt.

It is worth noting also that neither here nor in 'How to Kill' does Douglas eschew euphony. There is a good deal of rhyme, near-rhyme and metrical regularity. But their effect, I think, bearing that subject, is not in the least consolatory, but ironic and sardonic.

But is it delight, the entertaining of possibilities (here pitilessness) that would shock the virtuous philosopher? And do those rhythms and matching sounds still give delight? Delight is certainly a prime agent in the effecting of any poem's redress.

Poems give pleasure, even Owen's and Douglas's on those atrocious subjects. Pleasure of a peculiar kind, no doubt, but pleasure is still the word for it. Or satisfaction? The satisfaction of seeing something properly, fittingly, finally done? And what is it that is done? By one means or another, by one strategy or another, the poem, undeluded, quickens and alerts us to more ways of being human than we shall ever know in our small biographical selves.

If I say 'strategy' I do mean a direction and techniques more or less consciously decided upon by each poet in each poem; but those decisions will of course themselves be shaped by the poet's whole disposition of character in particular circumstance at the time. True strategies in poetry are heartfelt. And there are risks (needless to say) in both those adopted and epitomised by the two war poets Owen and Douglas. Owen, so full of pity and so bent on exciting it in his readers, risks depriving them of the shock of realisation in their own hearts, they may feel only the known, familiar and expected thing, and that will not be enough. And he risks an aestheticism of lushness, euphony and the beauty of sacrifice. Douglas, more profoundly unsettling, could not, I think, without serious poetic harm, have stayed out much longer living 'in gusto' in the zone of pitilessness. He risks the aestheticism of delight in everything equally, as though all phenomena were equal and none mattered.

Poetry must be agile, continually it must devise new ways to answer the changing circumstances and shapes of human life. In the act of doing so, in the very practice of words in a certain order, by the rhythms that engenders, by the making of sense, it excites an answering quickness in the reader, at the heart of which is the freedom to assent or contradict. The resources for poetry's agility lie deep in a steady survival, in a long tradition, in an identity which under how ever many different appearances is peculiarly sure of itself.

SOURCES:

Brecht's remarks on poetry will be found, in German, in the excellent anthology *Über Lyrik* (Suhrkamp, 1968); and many of them, in English, in my contribution to Brecht's *Poetry of Political Exile* (CUP, 2000). For Keith Douglas, poems and comments, see *The Complete Poems* (OUP, 1990).

Poetry of the Present

A poet must try to say what it feels like being human in a particular time and place. What living is like then.

A poem has to have a shape. It is not possible for it to have no shape. The shape may be more or less suitable and effective, but it is none the less a shape. A poem is not there until it has a shape. A poetic feeling, state, aspiration, disposition is, of itself, for anyone else in the world but the person feeling it, nothing. A state not shown, not bodied forth, not made palpable – that is, not given shape – is nothing so far as the outside world is concerned, it does not exist. It has to be realised.

By shape I mean particular words in a particular order (which will obey or determine a particular rhythm) set out in some arrangement on the page.

A distinction is often made between mechanical form and organic form. The terms are rather loaded, suggesting one ought to prefer the latter. 'Mechanical form' tends to mean that the form – the total shape, metrical pattern and arrangement – pre-exists the particular poem or poetic impulse. The sonnet shape, for example, has been available to European poets for about 700 years. A particular poetic impulse, inspiration, project, may be fitted into that pre-existent shape. 'Organic form' tends to mean that every poetic project must find its own uniquely suitable and novel shape. D.H. Lawrence will serve as an advocate of that view here. He wrote to Edward Marsh (18 August 1913): 'I have always tried to get an emotion out in its own course, without altering it.' The shape comes with the inspiration, the shape is the necessary, only possible, expression of that inspiration. Lawrence again, to Marsh (19 November 1913): 'This is the constant war, I reckon, between new expression and the habituated, mechanical transmitters and receivers of the human constitution.' Since life is ever-changing, the transmitters and receivers must change too. Poetry has to be agile. Mechanical form may then seem quite unsuitable; what was fixed once cannot help again. In this view, mechanical and organic are poles apart, quite irreconcilable, and any writer trying to say what life is like in the here and now must necessarily go for the new shape every time.

In practice, of course, no such absolute distinction operates. The iambic pentameter, itself a shape and a constituent part of a larger shape, has been an option for English poets since Chaucer. In that sense it is mechanical form. But glance again at the translations by Surrey and by Wyatt of the same Petrarch sonnet and it will be obvious how differently each moves in his iambic lines. I'll remind you that Keats, turning from Milton to Chatterton, said 'I wish to give myself up to other sensations.' In the following very familiar speech from *Macbeth* all the lines, except the first and the last, are full iambic pentameters, but the *sensation* of each is quite distinct:

>   She should have died hereafter;
> There would have been a time for such a word. –
> Tomorrow, and tomorrow, and tomorrow,
> Creeps in this petty pace from day to day,
> To the last syllable of recorded time;
> And all our yesterdays have lighted fools
> The way to dusty death. Out, out, brief candle!
> Life's but a walking shadow; a poor player,
> That struts and frets his hour upon the stage,
> And then is heard no more: it is a tale
> Told by an idiot, full of sound and fury,
> Signifying nothing.

Compare that with the exhanges between Pericles and Marina in the Recognition Scene (*Pericles*, V. I) or with these lines from the ending of the *The Winter's Tale*:

> PAULINA.   That she is living,
>   Were it but told you, should be hooted at
>   Like an old tale; but it appears she lives,
>   Though yet she speak not. Mark a little while. –
>   Please you to interpose, fair madam: kneel,
>   And pray your mother's blessing. – Turn, good lady;
>   Our Perdita is found.
> HERMIONE.   You gods, look down
>   And from your sacred vials pour your graces
>   Upon my daughter's head! – Tell me, mine own,
>   Where hast thou been preserv'd? where liv'd? how found?
>   Thy father's court?

The variety is lovely, and not hard to explain. It is the playing of rhythm, which we might call organic, over a metrical requirement, which we might call mechanical. The rhythm is how we naturally speak the lines, the metre is an agreed discipline of which the voice and the head and the heart are delicately aware and which, to good effect (the making of beauty) they obey or contradict.

On the whole classical, renaissance and many early 18th-century poets operated in fixed forms and saw no reason not to. They were willing to be governed by decorum and propriety, which is not as craven as it might sound. It simply means they were inclined to accommodate the particular poetic undertaking to a suitable pre-existent form. But since Romanticism (mid-18th century onwards) many writers have felt that they, or their poems, must devise shapes and forms of their own. Fifty years before Keats used the phrase, writers, and not just writers, had come to think themselves uniquely shaped and defined by 'the heart's affections'; a person's individuality, his or her authentic self, resided precisely in these affections, which is why Keats called them holy. Easy to suppose that a poem expressing these uniquely defining feelings must find its own shape. You might call this a private and sacred duty, or just another application of the doctrine of aptness, which any classical writer would subscribe to. Most obviously it resulted in a demand for freedom, for freer forms; and Romantic writers, looking around, soon found a goodly number of alternative, freer, more organic models. Among these were the Psalms, Ossian, Persian and Arabic verse and the sixth-century Greek poet Pindar (all, be it said, in translation). It does not matter how *correct* they were in their reading of these authors. Mostly, by later scholarly standards, they were not at all correct. And the translators themselves often more or less consciously embodied the enthusiasm for which, with their translations, they were supplying further encouragement and material. That was certainly the case with Ossian and James Macpherson. Pindar is interesting in that same respect. Thanks to Horace, who likened him to a rushing mighty river, he reached the mid-eighteenth century with a reputation for ungovernable genius, ecstatically dithyrambic. In fact, none of his dithyrambs had survived, and the actually very strict and complex metres of the poems that had, his Victory Odes, were not understood until the beginning of the twentieth century. Editors prior to that broke his lines and set out the poems much as they pleased, and, by design or not, the effect thus produced – very long poems, lines of wildly varying lengths – was indeed that of a river carving out its own necessary shape as it went along. Translators, if anything, only strengthened the impression of self-determining freedom. That is how the young Goethe read Pindar, why he made him a champion of his *Sturm und Drang* and wrote odes of his own in pindaric style that take the physical shape of wildly running feeling on the page. Not how correct the reading, but how inspiring, how productive, is what matters. Goethe, breaking through into the true voice of feeling, wanted shapes that would express that breakthrough, rhythms, lineation, disposition and movement of subject 'like Pindar's'. He imitated also Pindar's habit of fashioning powerful neologisms, ramming together word-pieces, in the epithets especially. German is as resourceful as Greek in this. A writer can make for the new moment its new word.

I began with Lawrence and in this question of the benefits (and risks) of organic form I'll consider now a writer whom, for a good while at least, he greatly admired, Walt Whitman. In his own theory and practice of 'poetry of the present' Lawrence acknowledged Whitman as origin and inspiration. They had this in common: the wish to give the rushing abundance and variety of life its proper due.

The premise, stated or not, is that life exceeds art. The abundance, variety and headlong momentum of life can never be adequately said in any poem. This is a fact to celebrate, not regret. The poem can live and thrive precisely there, in the celebration of its being continuously exceeded by the life that is its subject. As I said at the outset, it is not possible for a poem to have no shape, and every chosen and arrived-at shape is in some degree an act of fixing and containment. Some strains of verse have even made that their aim: to contain and fix, as though life could be nailed down and thus, like a butterfly with a pin through it, be preserved. But what Lawrence, Whitman and many others have wanted is to arrive at forms that will continuously signal life's excess, whose very function, as form, is to show forth what cannot be fixed or contained, actually to embody and make palpable life's neverending streaming away.

For convenience, I shall distinguish two elements in life's constant exceeding of any work of art. One is abundance, the other is quickness. This is very rough-and-ready, not at all watertight, but it will serve a purpose to consider Whitman as the poet of abundance and Lawrence as the poet of quickness.

Whitman took a large country (modern America) and an even larger ego (his own) for subjects, and inevitably had his poetic hands full. A long line was called for, a line free to lengthen as long as it liked, to encompass all it could and by its rhythms to suggest yet more. He himself called his lines 'omnivorous' (*Leaves of Grass*, p. 67), they had stomach for anything and everything, and that, at the end of the nineteenth century, was a very salutary manifesto. He opened his verse to modernity, his lines are capacious and elastic enough to accommodate the plethora of objects and dictions that narrower, less generous poetics had excluded. For no subject is of itself 'unpoetic' (none is 'poetic' either), all possible subjects are equally fit for poetry. That means, of course, that no words, phrases, locutions are, of themselves, fitter for the poem than others. All words are equal, they can be employed wherever it suits. This is a vastly liberating move, a great democratising, a further, more inclusive, application of Wordsworth's opening of poetry to 'the real language of men'. There is room and a welcome in Whitman's lines for all the traditional three levels of poetic discourse, the high, middle and low; for the psalmic, the technically precise, the demotic, the casual, the sententious, the banal. Whitman's ambition was 'to exalt the present and the real, / To teach the average man the glory of his daily walk and trade' (p. 171). This is ideal America, the great all-comprehending democratic celebration, the dignifying, the raising up as fit to be looked at and admired of the multiplicity, passion and value of ordinary lives. The lines want a large breath for a task as glorious and vast as this, rhythms like those of a secular liturgy, and a constant pointing beyond, to the more and more that no lines of verse will ever encompass. As here, in his singing the variety of work, and the workers themselves all singing:

> I hear America singing, the varied carols I hear,
> Those of mechanics, each one singing his as it should be blithe
>   and strong,
> The carpenter singing his as he measures his plank or beam,
> The mason singing his as he makes ready for work, or leaves off
>   work,
> The boatman singing what belongs to him in his boat, the deckhand
>   singing on the steamboat deck,
> The shoemaker singing as he sits on his bench, the hatter singing
>   as he stands,
> The wood-cutter's song, the ploughboy's on his way in the morning,
>   or at noon intermission or at sundown,
> The delicious singing of the mother, or of the young wife at work,
>   or of the girl sewing or washing,
> Each singing what belongs to him or her and to none else...
>   (pp. 9-10)

He celebrates the huge geographical extent of America and the movement and activity all the length and breadth of it, and from it, under the Atlantic, to Europe and back:

> See, steamers steaming through my poems,
> See, in my poems immigrants continually coming and landing,
> See, in arriere, the wigwam, the trail, the hunter's hut, the flat-boat,
>   the maize-leaf, the claim, the rude fence, and the backwoods
>   village,
> See, on the one side the Western Sea and on the other side the
>   Eastern Sea, how they advance and retreat upon my poems
>   as upon their own shores,
> See, pastures and forests in my poems – see, animals wild and tame
>   – see, beyond the Kaw, countless herds of buffalo feeding
>   on short curly grass,
> See, in my poems, cities, solid, vast, inland, with paved streets, with
>   iron and stone edifices, ceaseless vehicles, and commerce,
> See, the many-cylindered steam printing-press – see, the electric
>   telegraph stretching across the continent,
> See, through Atlantica's depths pulses American Europe reaching,
>   pulses of Europe duly returned...
>   (p. 22)

He extends his humanity in sympathy into all forms of animal, vegetable and mineral life, or they partake of him:

> I find I incorporate gneiss, coal, long-threaded moss, fruits, grains,
>   esculent roots,
> And am stuccoed with quadrupeds and birds all over.
>   (p. 50)

The ego devising these capacious lines is itself 'infinite and omnigenous'. It accommodates all things and, so doing, necessarily lives in contradictions:

> Do I contradict myself?
> Very well then, I contradict myself,
> (I am large, I contain multitudes).
> (p. 76)

Life is like that, in the multitude and in diversity there is bound to be ceaseless contradiction. The ego partaking of all that, being of the same stuff then, will not falsify itself by resolving or denying the contradictions.

Whitman is interested in all things – 'Whatever interests the rest interests me...' (p. 66) – extends his sympathy into all things and furthermore – a grand claim – sets himself as omnipresent witness, humanity's martyr. Ecce homo: Walt Whitman!

> All this I swallow, it tastes good, I like it well, it becomes mine,
> I am the man, I suffered, I was there.
>
> The disdain and calmness of martyrs,
> The mother of old, condemned for a witch, burnt with dry wood, her children gazing on,
> The hounded slave that flags in the race, leans by the fence, blowing, covered with sweat,
> The twinges that sting like needles his legs and neck, the murderous buckshot and the bullets,
> All these I feel or am.
> (p. 57)

The philosophy of Whitman's verse, the imperative that drives him into such omnivorous lines, is a Nietzschean saying yea to everything that lives. Some of his lists are remarkable for the jostling in them of very discrepant things, things one might be glad of, things one would normally regret or deprecate, all coming pell-mell without discrimination:

> The quadroon girl is sold at the auction-stand, the drunkard nods by the bar-room stove,
> The machinist rolls up his sleeves, the policeman travels his beat, the gate-keeper marks who pass,
> The young fellow drives the express-wagon (I love him though I do not know him)...
> (p. 35)

Whitman knows perfectly well that he is doing this:

> I am he attesting sympathy...
> I am not the poet of goodness only, I do not decline to be the poet of wickedness also.
>
> What blurt is this about virtue and about vice?
> Evil propels me and reform of evil propels me, I stand indifferent,
> My gait is no fault-finder's or rejecter's gait,
> I moisten the roots of all that has grown.
> (pp. 42-43)

He is chameleon poet, not virtuous philosopher. It is a large part of the liberation, the huge widening of subject and diction, the openness, without prejudice, to all. His celebration encompasses all things, and on that brew he becomes exalted.

That excitement seems to me more than a bit suspect. Not the setting side by side in a list of good and bad. Life is like that and a poet can administer a salutary shock by such unmediated juxtapositions. It is the excitement, the celebration, I have my doubts about. That mode does *not* give people their due. Because the due that people are owed was then and is now not always undiscriminating celebration ('All this I swallow, it tastes good, I like it well') but, very often, pity, and an active rage on their behalf. And I have even more doubts about the quality of his witness. It seems to me an abuse of, or wrong claim made for, poetic empathy, to confuse it with actually being there in the flesh. Some claims to witness seem to me completely spurious and disreputable. I can think of many situations about which nobody should say 'I was the man. I suffered. I was there' unless he was quite literally the man and was there and did suffer. The facility of the imagination – easy to imagine things – brings with it sometimes a facility of witness. Among the several sardonic inner voices a poet at work should hearken to is the one that asks: 'Do you actually know what you are talking about?' Whitman slips too easily into the voice of witness and into an idealising exaltation which, for all his insistence on individual trades, incidents or places, in fact very often overlooks particularity. A pity, since the lines he devised could in practice, had he wished it, accommodate the most recalcitrant and abrasive particularity. But these lines, excellent for his strengths, encourage this weakness too, a weakness that comes with the insistently celebratory intent.

The long line, or the line that can swell or shrink, breathe out or in, as the need of the moment dictates, has its roots in the rhythms of the Authorised Version, particularly the Psalms and the Song of Songs. Christopher Smart in his *Jubilate Agno* and Blake in his prophetic books hark back there. The long line I mentioned in my first lecture, the fourteen-syllable line devised by Chapman to translate the *Iliad*, is nothing like so capacious or versatile. First because of its fixed iambic metre, secondly because of its tendency to fall into two unequal halves (8 + 6), which read like those of the traditional ballad stanza. (The long line must run its course, we must feel a breath sustained right through it necessarily.) Chapman's fourteeners are also, be it said, much less capable of variety than are the Greek hexameters which they translate. Democratised by Whitman, made fit for the demotic voice, the long free-verse line runs through much of American poetry to the present day. C.K. Williams, for example, handles it to very good effect.

The advantages of such a line, as I have tried to demonstrate, are many and great. They amount to a freedom to be more comprehensive and to track the real voices, pulse and rhythms of life more closely. I don't say the long free-verse line is the only means of doing that, but it certainly has a fitness to do that. The risks in the line are as obvious as its promise. It encourages prolixity, it is tolerant of looseness, inconsquentiality, the accidental, the mere list. In those very risks, its advocates might say, it is more like life. An appearance of haste, scrappiness, randomness may be a desirable aim. But the crux is the word 'appearance'. Poetry works through appearances, and they have to be artfully done. Real scrappiness, randomness etc are undesirable, because ineffectual. It must also be said of the Whitmanesque line, and not just Whitman's, that it is a great encourager of blather. What should be the wind of Pentecost blowing through it, is often only wind.

Lawrence's essay *Poetry of the Present* (1919), intended as a preface to his collection *Look! We have come through!*, actually served to introduce his *New Poems* in America in 1920. I will summarise the argument of that essay.

Lawrence considers our traditional poetry to be either a recollection of the past or an aspiration towards the future. But his own interest is in what he calls the *terra incognita* of the the present, of now, of the instant, and in a poetry that would be capable of rendering that. He ascribes finality, perfection, consumateness to the poetries of the past and the future. Their treasured masterpieces are 'the gem-like lyrics of Shelley and Keats', which were built of the formal patterning of rhyme and regular metre. Lawrence's opening thesis seems to me dubious, but much more important and far more persuasive is his characterisation of poetry of the present. The sentences themselves give the feeling of what is wanted:

> But there is another kind of poetry: the poetry of that which is at hand: the immediate present. In the immediate present there is no perfection, no consummation, nothing finished. The strands are all flying, quivering, intermingling into the web, the waters are shaking the moon. There is no round, consummate moon on the face of running water, nor on the face of the unfinished tide...
>
> Life, the ever-present, knows no finality, no finished crystallisation. The perfect rose is only a running flame, emerging and flowing off, and never in any sense at rest, static, finished. Herein lies its transcendent loveliness. The whole tide of all life and all time suddenly heaves, and appears before us as an apparition, a revelation. We look at the very white quick of nascent creation...
>
> There is poetry of this immediate present, instant poetry, as well as poetry of the infinite past and the infinite future. The seething poetry of the incarnate Now is supreme, beyond even the everlasting gems of the before and after. In its quivering momentaneity it surpasses the crystalline pearl-hard jewels, the poems of the eternities. Do not ask for the qualities of the unfading timeless gems. Ask for the whiteness which is the seethe of mud, ask for that incipient putrescence which is the skies falling, ask for the never-pausing, never-ceasing life itself. There must be mutation, swifter than iridescence, haste not rest, come-and-go, not fixity, inconclusiveness, immediacy, the quality of life itself, without dénouement or close. There must be the rapid momentaneous association of things which meet and pass on the for ever incalculable journey of creation: everything left in its own rapid, fluid relationship with the rest of things.

The first poet waking wholly to the present, says Lawrence, was Whitman.

> This is the unrestful, ungraspable poetry of the sheer present, poetry whose very permanency lies in its wind-like transit. Whitman's is

the best poetry of this kind. Without beginning and without end, without any base and pediment, it sweeps past for ever, like a wind that is for ever in passage, and unchainable.
(*Selected Literary Criticism*, pp. 85-87)

The only form for a poetry of the present is free verse, after Whitman's fashion. 'He is so near the quick.' Free verse cannot be merely regular verse, chopped up. It must come new every time, from within, to answer the occasion. Since the present moment is necessarily unfinished, since it is, as Lawrence says, the wellhead, always in flux, a poetry seeking to track it must approach the chaos out of which the defined shapes of things are only just emerging. Lawrence says we fear Whitman; and that must be because, as he says elsewhere, there is in us both 'the desire for chaos, and the fear of chaos' (*SLC*, 92).

The essay, and other scattered remarks, amount to a clear aim: to convey in verse the quickness of the present moment; and a conviction that only genuinely free verse will serve.

The realisation of the doctrine came less in Lawrence's *Look! We Have Come Through!* than in his collection *Birds, Beasts and Flowers* (1923). Several of the poems in the collection return to the same subject: fig trees and figs; almond trees; bats; tortoises; goats. And within any single poem there is a good deal of quite deliberate coming again and again at an essentially elusive centre; never an exact repetition, rather a trying again, a rephrasing and modification in the bid to come closer. In 'Sicilian Cyclamens', for example, he approaches the flowers through images of them first as toads, then as greyhounds, then as hares. And it is not that one image replaces another, as being more apt. None quite lapses, all remain possible, the effect is cumulative. I should have to quote the whole poem to illustrate this adequately. But here are the greyhounds, still harking back to the toads ('out of earth', 'stone-engendered') and anticipating their quarry, the hares:

> The shaking aspect of the sea
> And man's defenceless bare face
> And cyclamens putting their ears back.
> Long, pensive, slim-muzzled greyhound buds
> Dreamy, not yet present,
> Drawn out of earth
> At his toes.

> Dawn-rose
> Sub-delighted, stone-engendered
> Cyclamens, young cyclamens
> Arching
> Waking, pricking their ears
> Like delicate very-young greyhound bitches
> Half-yawning at the open, inexperienced
> Vista of day,
> Folding back their soundless petalled ears.
>
> Greyhound bitches
> Bending their rosy muzzles pensive down,
> And breathing soft, unwilling to wake to the new day
> Yet sub-delighted.

The effect of this strategy (it *is* a strategy) is to make the subject feel inexhaustible and essentially intractable. All that metamorphosis, and still it needs more! Failure itself points up the excess of the living subject over the poet's powers. Of course, we have to be persuaded that the poet *has* powers. Incompetence will not show up the elusive quickness of the subject, only the writer's incompetence. But since Lawrence at his best is very good indeed, the sense he excites in us that the subject exceeds even him, is a mark of his success in doing it justice.

Many of the poems – 'Bibbles', 'Elephant', for example – are very long. That is of a piece with, and sometimes of course actually caused by, the strategy of repetition and trying again. But their length also allows great variation in tone, texture, pace and – it has to be said – vitality. Many of the poems lapse more than once en route into flatness, banality or, worst of all, intrusive commentary and hectoring. Hölderlin thought the unpoetic had a proper place and function in the economy of a long poem, and Lawrence, in his free verse, clearly allowed or could not help the same. In his fiction he works similarly. We might say it is very hit and miss, very careless, inconsistent, unsustained. Or we could say – this might be sophistry, it might be charity – that the lowerings and lapses of vitality are a true and necesasry part of the whole long poem's bidding again and again to get near the never diminished energy of its subject. We feel him coming near the quick (as he said of Whitman: 'He is so near the quick') in part through the negative experience of his lapses.

It must not be thought that Lawrence is trying to describe the birds, beast and flowers that give his poems their titles. When I say he is trying again and again to get nearer and nearer to the quick, I mean he is trying to convey his whole experience of the object in question, and that is a dynamic interacting between a human consciousness and the autonomous thing in the outside world. The liveliness and abundance to be conveyed are generated precisely there in that encounter and reciprocation. This is very obvious in 'Man and Bat' and in the justly famous poem 'Snake'; but it is there too at all moments when, in the necessary striving to say what the encounter is *like* he reaches for comparisons, develops a response through imagery or through an act of memory. What the object or, better, the encounter with the object, excites, is the imagination and memory of the human being in it. Thus in 'Medlars and Sorb-Apples', the eerie conjuring up of the lanes of hell:

> Sorb-apples, medlars with dead crowns.
> I say, wonderful are the hellish experiences,
> Orphic, delicate
> Dionysos of the Underworld.
>
> A kiss, and a spasm of farewell, a moment's orgasm of rupture,
> Then along the damp road alone, till the next turning.
> And there, a new partner, a new parting, a new unfusing into twain,
> A new gasp of further isolation,
> A new intoxication of loneliness, among decaying, frost-cold leaves.
>
> Going down the strange lanes of hell, more and more intensely alone,
> The fibres of the heart parting one after the other
> And yet the soul continuing, naked-footed, ever more vividly
>   embodied
> Like a flame blown whiter and whiter
> In a deeper and deeper darkness
> Ever more exquisite, distilled in separation.
>
> So, in the strange retorts of medlars and sorb-apples
> The distilled essence of hell
> The exquisite odour of leave-taking.
>   *Jamque vale!*
> Orpheus, and the winding, leaf-clogged, silent lanes of hell.

And in 'Tortoise Shout', the extraordinary sequence of 'I remember...': the various kinds of utterance, all more or less terrifying, that ever struck home in him. I'll begin half way through:

> I remember the first time, out of a bush in the darkness, a nightingale's
>   piercing cries and gurgles startled the depths of my soul;
> I remember the scream of a rabbit as I went through a wood at
>   midnight;
> I remember the heifer in her heat, blorting and blorting through
>   the hours, persistent and irrepressible;
> I remember my first terror hearing the howl of weird, amorous cats;
> I remember the scream of a terrified, injured horse, the sheet-
>   lightning,
> And running away from the sound of a woman in labour, something
>   like an owl whooing,
> And listening inwardly to the first bleat of a lamb,
> The first wail of in infant,
> And my mother singing to herself,
> And the first tenor singing of the passionate throat of a young collier,
>   who has long since drunk himself to death,
> The first elements of foreign speech
> On wild dark lips.

Such memories are a large part of a person's self. The poem quickens them, liveliness is achieved..

There is a gap, inevitably, between the exciting ambition of the essay – to convey, without fixing it, the Heraclitean moving and flowing of life – and the execution in many of the poems. But in his successes – in 'Kangaroo', 'Bare Almond-Trees', 'Almond Blossom', for example – in the flashes of success, not just in the poems but in essays, letters, stories and novels too, Lawrence is quicker in those moments, closer to life in its making and passing, than perhaps any writer has ever been.

'The letter killeth, but the spirit giveth life.' I suppose all poets write with that in mind. The injunction seems clear: go for the spirit. But in poetry, as I said at the outset, without the letter there is no spirit, or none that is able to be felt by anyone else. Without the words, the words in a particular order, fitted into a syntax, engendering a rhythm, making sense, without the letter (understood like that) there is nothing that can have any effect. The letter used wrongly does indeed kill; it fixes; where there was life (the spirit) it makes a dead thing; the syntax remains a skeleton, life refuses to inhabit it. And that is really the continuous and necessary struggle in verse, between fixity and fluidity, between the way of death and the way of life. And in that struggle, in which the very life of the spirit is at stake, the letter is all, and may petrify or animate. I guess there would be agreement that liveliness, trueness to life in its movement and excess, is the heart and soul of the poem, that without which it cannot work. Whitman wholly and Lawrence for much of the time thought free verse (organic form) the only way to go after that liveliness, and many poets then and since have thought the same. Still more, however, from the very beginnings to the present day, have thought the rhymes and stanzas and regular metres of mechanical form will do as well or better.

Rilke is of interest here. In his *Neue Gedichte* (1907-08) there are a dozen or so poems on birds, beasts and flowers, and he was certainly as anxious as Lawrence to render their liveliness and the lively interaction of himself with them, not to fix and annihilate it. He was employed at the time in Paris as secretary to the sculptor Auguste Rodin, whom he greatly admired (and dedicated the second part of the *Neue Gedichte* to him). Rilke learned from Rodin the art of looking: of looking and looking until the subject was transferable into words, as Rodin's model was into clay, marble or bronze. Which sounds very much like transference into fixity. But Rodin's sculptures are remarkable not just for their solidity but also for his constant aspiration in them to contradict the inevitable immobility and weightiness of the medium with the appearance of movement, flight, evanescence. In his sculptures (and even more so in his rapid and erotically charged drawings) he poses the human body at what Rilke would later call 'the point of turn', which is the moment between a dancer's landing and leaping, or when a swallow or a fulmar halts on the air for one split second, and veers away again. Movement held up long enough for us to know it as movement. Rilke's collection was called *New Poems* because, instructed by Rodin, whose doctrine was daily hard work, he cut free in them from a Romantic dependence on inspiration and went off to the Jardin des Plantes to contemplate birds, beasts and flowers, until the words for them came. The shapes he gave them were not in the least free verse, but rhyming quatrains, sonnets, regular metres. Like Rodin, he wanted to make something substantial, something you could, so to speak, walk round and view from all angles, and it would be fit to be looked at. Again, that sounds very fixed.

But he countered that risk with an almost programmatic enjambement, with a running over the line-endings where the rhymes (the fixing sounds) were placed. And with much euphony and many interconnecting assonances, he gave the poems a vibrancy and a lively texturing, akin to the being of the flamingo, panther, blue or pink hydrangea itself. In his treatment of the many other subjects too – works of sculpture or architecture, episodes from the bible or from legend, human figures on the street or in society, lovers, a girl at her window – in all, none of them in free verse, there is no stasis, no fixity, but a restlessness, movement, a fine contradicting and overrunning of the formal requirements of the verse.

In his *Sonnets to Orpheus* it is even more the case. Rilke wrote these sonnets – fifty-five of them – between 2 and 23 February 1922 in the tower at Muzot, whilst and immediately after finishing the *Duino Elegies*, a glorious alternative and aftermath. They are addressed to Orpheus, who, for his knowledge of the kingdoms of life and of death; his ability to move the stones and charm the beasts; and the sacrificial strewing of his body across the landscape by the jealous maenads, may be understood as the pagan patron saint of metamorphosis. And they were dedicated to the memory of Wera Ouckama Knoop, a dancer, the daughter of a friend, who had died only recently at the age of nineteen. The sonnets are alive with the movement of dance, the inventiveness the dancer needs to cast and recast the body expressively, they enact the metamorphoses suffered, effected and championed by Orpheus. Rilke himself commented on his handling of the sonnet form:

> I keep calling them sonnets. Though they are the freest and, so to speak, the most mutated things conceivable in that usually so still and stable form. But precisely that: to mutate the sonnet, to lift it, in a certain sense to run with it in my hands without destroying it, that was, on this occasion, my peculiar trial and commission.

Rilke rhymes in all manner of schemes; his lines may be long or short, iambic or – unusually for the sonnet – dactylic; feeling and argument are disposed through a great variety of arrangements of the fourteen lines. But the form remains intact, these are still sonnets, they mutate in the liveliest manner in something fixed. The dancer Rudolf Nureyev, very sure of his own essential identity, said in an interview soon after his arrival in the west that he wanted 'to find new ways of moving'. And that is what these sonnets do. Sure of themselves as sonnets, secure in that identity, they delight in change. Several have as their subjects the very principle of change; or they celebrate such phenomena as music, dance, running water, breath, fire, the wind, agents or embodiments of change.

Strict forms are at least as capable as free verse is of engendering the feeling of freedom and closeness to the onward rushing and changes of life. The point does not need labouring. Hölderlin in his odes and elegies employed metres deriving from classical Greek which were far more demanding than the rhyming in quatrains and tercets. Yet no poet ever raised and liberated the spirit more. Hypotaxis is one of his strategies to that end, sentences riding in strict metre over a dozen or more long lines of verse, a palpable rising and overflowing from line to line, from stanza to stanza, on and on. And this cumulative rhythm, his very signature as a poet, is achieved precisely in 'the loving quarrel' (his phrase) with prosodic requirement. The law is there to make possible a productive fighting, law makes transgression an option and licence a risk and a delight. There are many applications of Blake's famous dictum 'Without contraries is no progression'. The dialectic of strict form with the pentecostal spirit blowing through it is one.

I called this lecture *Poetry of the Present*, alluding to Lawrence's essay which is at the heart of it. In conclusion I want to emphasise that all poetry, when it works, is of the present. In reality there is no past or future in the poem. By one means or another (fixed or free) it brings about presence, immanent presence. Things absent in past or future are made present by our reading of conventional black signs on a white page. As we read, something is going on in us, something is coming into being. There is a realisation; the total economy, all the strategies of the poem bring it about. Lowell was right to say that a poem is an event, not the record of an event. And Auden, in that poem ('In Memory of W.B. Yeats') in which he asserts that poetry makes nothing happen, asserts with greater persuasiveness that it is 'a way of happening'. That happening is so intensely present we may weep or laugh aloud or shudder in terror – at what? At something 'only' there in our consciousness as we read. Such realisation is very presence.

That is the chief good and usefulness of poetry. It persuades or jolts us into what Lawrence called 'a new effort of attention' (*SLC*, p. 90), it fills us with the achievement of that attention. There is no gainsaying the charge of poetry, nor how valuable it feels. It is a condition of being, not of having. It can't be *had*, it is intrinsically resistant to acquisitiveness. And by being alert and truthful and upholding contradictory possibilities, asserting homegeneity, championing a lively pluralism, acknowledging the essential irreducibility and intractability of life, poetry is the living contradiction of political speech and a gesture of defiance in the face of all reductive, co-ordinating and tyrannical political systems. We are, when we read poetry, during the reading of the poem and lingeringly for some while after, more wakeful, alert and various in our humanity than in our practical lives we are mostly allowed to be. Achieving that, in vital cooperation with the reader, a poet has done the most he or she is qualified to do. Any further stage, any conversion of this alerted present state into action, into behaviour, is the responsibility of the citizen. And the poet, like the reader, is always a citizen.

SOURCES:

Lawrence's letters and essays are referred to in D.H. Lawrence, *Selected Literary Criticism* (Mercury Books, 1961); his poems in Volume One of *The Complete Poems of D.H. Lawrence* (Heinemann, 1972). Whitman's poems are referred to in *Leaves of Grass* (Everyman, 1943).

NEWCASTLE/ BLOODAXE POETRY SERIES

Elizabeth Bishop:
Poet of the Periphery
edited by LINDA ANDERSON & JO SHAPCOTT

Elizabeth Bishop is one of the greatest poets of the 20th century. When she died in 1979, she had only published four collections, yet had won virtually every major American literary award, including the Pulitzer Prize. She maintained close friendships with poets such as Marianne Moore and Robert Lowell, and her work has always been highly regarded by other writers. In surveys of British poets carried out in 1984 and 1994 she emerged as a surprising major choice or influence for many, from Andrew Motion and Craig Raine to Kathleen Jamie and Lavinia Greenlaw.

A virtual orphan from an early age, Elizabeth Bishop was brought up by relatives in New England and Nova Scotia. The tragic circumstances of her life – from alcoholism to repeated experiences of loss in her relationships with women – nourished an outsider's poetry notable both for its reticence and tentativeness. She once described a feeling that 'everything is interstitial' and reminds us in her poetry – in a way that is both radical and subdued – that understanding is at best provisional and that most vision is peripheral.

Since her death, a definitive edition of Elizabeth Bishop's *Complete Poems* (1983) has been published, along with *The Collected Prose* (1984), her letters in *One Art* (1994), her paintings in *Exchanging Hats* (1996) and Brett C. Millier's important biography (1993). In America, there have been numerous critical studies and books of academic essays, but in Britain only studies by Victoria Harrison (1995) and Anne Stevenson (1998) have done anything to raise Bishop's critical profile.

Elizabeth Bishop: Poet of the Periphery is the first collection of essays on Bishop to be published in Britain, and draws on work presented at the first UK Elizabeth Bishop conference, held at Newcastle University. It brings together papers by both academic critics and leading poets, including Michael Donaghy, Vicki Feaver, Jamie McKendrick, Deryn Rees-Jones and Anne Stevenson. Academic contributors include Professor Barbara Page of Vassar College, home of the Elizabeth Bishop Papers.

ISBN 1 85224 556 5   216 x 138 mm   208 pages   £12 paperback

ALSO FROM BLOODAXE BOOKS

DAVID CONSTANTINE
Collected Poems
POETRY BOOK SOCIETY RECOMMENDATION

David Constantine is one the finest poets writing in English. His poetry stands outside the current literary climate, and like the work of the European poets who have nourished him, it is informed by a profoundly humane vision of the world. Its mood is often one of unease, elegiac or comically edged, barbed with pain or tinged with pleasure. His poems hold a worried and restless balance between celebration and anxiety, restraint and longing.

His *Collected Poems* spans three decades, including work from seven previous Bloodaxe titles and two limited editions, as well as a whole collection of new poems.

'The mood is both tender and desperate, with something of the uncanny in its blend of the recognisably human and apparently Other... His religious regard for the world (not the same thing as religious conviction) produces a strange translation of its ordinary terms. Its colours and joys and terrors are heightened as though by fever, yet at the same time brought into clearer focus' – SEAN O'BRIEN, *Poetry Review*

'Constantine's peculiar vision is an uneasy blend of the exquisite and the everyday...the beatific, the ordinary, the rebarbative even, are almost indistinguishable...Overwhelmingly the poems are intelligent and well-turned, setting out the tensions between innocence and experience with fine control' – ELIZABETH LOWRY, *TLS*

ISBN 1 85224 667 7   234 x 156 mm   388 pages   £12 paperback

David Constantine was born in 1944 in Salford, Lancashire. He read Modern Languages at Wadham College, Oxford, and lectured in German at Durham from 1969 to 1981 and at Oxford from 1981 to 2000. He is a freelance writer and translator, a Fellow of the Queen's College, Oxford, and co-editor with Helen Constantine of *Modern Poetry in Translation*. He lives in Oxford and Scilly.

His first book of poems, *A Brightness to Cast Shadows* (Bloodaxe Books, 1980), was widely acclaimed. His second collection, *Watching for Dolphins* (Bloodaxe Books, 1983), won the 1984 Alice Hunt Bartlett Prize, and his academic study, *Early Greek Travellers and the Hellenic Ideal* (Cambridge University Press, 1984), won the first Runciman Prize in 1985. His first novel, *Davies*, was published by Bloodaxe in 1985, and his first book of stories, *Back at the Spike* by Ryburn Publishing in 1994. *Fields of Fire*, his biography of Sir William Hamilton, was published by Weidenfeld & Nicolson in 2001.

His third collection, *Madder* (Bloodaxe Books, 1987), a Poetry Book Society Recommendation, won the Southern Arts Literature Prize. The French edition of *Madder*, translated by Yves Bichet as *Sorlingues* (Éditions La Dogana, 1992), won the Prix Rhône-Alpes du Livre. His *Selected Poems* (Bloodaxe Books, 1991) was a Poetry Book Society Recommendation. *Caspar Hauser: a poem in nine cantos* (Bloodaxe Books, 1994) was followed by *The Pelt of Wasps* (Bloodaxe Books, 1998), and *Something for the Ghosts* (Bloodaxe Books, 2002), shortlisted for the Whitbread Poetry Award.

He has published translations of poetry and prose by German, French and Greek writers. He was joint winner of the European Translation Prize in 1998 for his translation of Friedrich Hölderlin's *Selected Poems* (Bloodaxe, 1990; new edition, 1996), published a critical introduction to the poetry of Hölderlin (OUP, 1988), and translated Hölderlin's versions of Sophocles' *Oedipus* and *Antigone* as *Hölderlin's Sophocles* (Bloodaxe, 2001). His translation of Hans Magnus Enzensberger's *Lighter Than Air* (Bloodaxe, 2002) won the Poetry Society's Corneliu M Popescu Prize for European Poetry Translation in 2003. He has also translated Goethe's novel *Elective Affinities* (OUP, World's Classics, 1994), Kleist's *Selected Writings* (Dent, 1997) and Goethe's *Faust* (forthcoming in Penguin Classics). The Bloodaxe Contemporary French Poets series includes his translations of (with Helen Constantine) *Spaced, Displaced* by Henri Michaux (1992) and (with Mark Treharne) *Under Clouded Skies / Beauregard* by Philippe Jaccottet (1994).

A Living Language is published at the same time as his *Collected Poems* (Bloodaxe Books, 2004).